THE

QUARTERLY

EDITED BY

GORDON LISH

THE QUARTERLY SHOUTS ITS WARMEST WELCOME
TO NEW COVER-DESIGNER CHIP KIDD—
AND JUST AS LOUDLY HOLLERS ITS HEARTIEST THANKS
TO ORIGINAL COVER-DESIGNER LORRAINE LOUIE!
(BUT, HUSH, HUSH, NOW WE HAVE TO WHISPER—
HAPPIEST OF HELLOS TO BABY ANNA MICHELLE.)

This magazine strives for every evidence of evenhandedness in all its dealings, and is especially keen to exhibit its indifference to literary celebrity, great or small.

Apart from our having to succumb to the physics of actual objects taken as a group and, therefore, our having to enforce a sequence to the entries that constitute the contents of an issue, we do what we can to suppress the impression of distinctions. Hence, of course, the occasion to offer the foregoing sentences—given that *The Quarterly* now elects to interrupt its policy in order that it might acquit itself of a call to attention for the piece that opens Q13's first section.

The title is "Spin." The author is Tim O'Brien. The concern is war. The story is taken from O'Brien's forthcoming work of fiction, *The Things They Carried*, due out from Houghton Mifflin/Seymour Lawrence this spring. When the editor of this magazine was choosing fiction for *Esquire* magazine, he chose a certain number of pages from O'Brien's novel *Going After Cacciato*. To be sure, the editor would have chosen all the pages of that novel had he been able to do so. These many years thereafter, nothing has changed—the editor of *The Quarterly* would turn over to Tim O'Brien all the furniture of *The Quarterly* if Tim O'Brien wanted it—and the prayer that Tim O'Brien's nights be ever easier.

THE
QUARTERLY

13 / SPRING 1990

VINTAGE BOOKS

A DIVISION OF RANDOM HOUSE, INC.

NEW YORK

The Quarterly (issn: 1:0893-3103) is edited by Gordon Lish
and is published March, June, September, and December
by Vintage Books, a division of Random House, Inc.,
201 E. 50th Street, New York, NY 10022. Subscriptions—
four issues at $36 US, $47 Canadian, $42 US overseas—
and address changes should be sent to the attention of
Subscription Office, 28th Floor. Orders received by
January 31 start with March number; by April 30, June number;
by July 31, September number; by October 31, December number.
See page 247 for purchase of back numbers.

Management by Ellen F. Torron

The Quarterly welcomes the opportunity to read work
of every character, and is especially concerned to keep
itself an open forum. Manuscripts must be accompanied by
the customary return materials, and should be addressed to
The Editor, The Quarterly, 201 East 50th Street, New York,
NY 10022. The Quarterly makes the utmost effort to offer
its response to manuscripts no later than one week
subsequent to receipt. Opinions expressed herein are not
necessarily those of the Editor or of the Publisher.

isbn: 0-679-72893-7

Design by Andrew Roberts
Editorial Assistance by Rick Whitaker
Installation by Denise Stewart

The Hob Broun Prize for 1989 is awarded to
Yannick Murphy for "The Beauty in Bulls," which fiction
appeared in Q9. The award is given annually and is
administered by The Quarterly for Mr. and Mrs. Heywood Hale Broun
in memory of the literary artist whose name the award bears.
Where this sentence stands there had been a sentence asking God
for Dom Leone's health, but now it is the keeping of Dom Leone's soul
that we must ask God for—for Dom Leone died, of cancer,
on 27 November 1989. He was twenty-nine years old.

Manufactured in the United States of America

THE
QUARTERLY

He wanted to be amplified across the universe

REPETITION
POINT OF VIEW

Spin

There was no music. Most of the hamlet had burned down, including her house, which was now smoke, and the girl danced with her eyes half closed, her feet bare. She was maybe fourteen. She had black hair and brown skin. "Why's she dancing?" Azar said. We searched through the wreckage but there wasn't much to find. Rat Kiley caught a chicken for dinner. Lieutenant Cross radioed up to the gunships and told them to go away. The girl danced mostly on her toes. She took tiny steps in the dirt in front of her house, sometimes making a slow twirl, sometimes smiling to herself. "Why's she dancing?" Azar said, and Henry Dobbins said it didn't matter why, she just was. Later we found her family in the house. They were dead and badly burned. It wasn't a big family: an infant and an old woman and a woman whose age was hard to tell. When we dragged them out, the girl kept dancing. She put the palms of her hands against her ears, which must've meant something, and she danced sideways for a short while, and then backwards. She did a graceful movement with her hips. "Well, I don't get it," Azar said. The smoke from the hootches smelled like straw. It moved in patches across the village square, not thick anymore, sometimes just faint ripples like fog. There were dead pigs, too. The girl went up onto her toes and made a slow turn and danced through the smoke. Her face had a dreamy look, quiet and composed. A while later, when we moved out of the hamlet, she was still dancing. "Probably some weird ritual," Azar said, but Henry Dobbins looked back and said, no, the girl just liked to dance.

That night, after we'd marched away from the smoking village, Azar mocked the girl's dancing. He did funny jumps and spins. He put the palms of his hands against his ears and danced sideways for a while, and then backwards, and then did an erotic thing with his hips. But Henry Dobbins, who moved gracefully for such a big man, took Azar from behind and lifted him up high and carried him over to a deep well and asked if he wanted to be dumped in.

Azar said no.

"All right, then," Henry Dobbins said, "dance right."

The war wasn't all terror and violence. Sometimes things could almost get sweet. For instance, I remember a little boy with a plastic leg. I remember how he hopped over to Azar and asked for a chocolate bar—"GI number one," the kid said—and Azar laughed and handed over the chocolate. When the boy hopped away, Azar clucked his tongue sadly. "One leg, for chrissake. Some poor fucker ran out of ammo."

I remember Mitchell Sanders sitting quietly in the shade of an old banyan tree. He was using a thumbnail to pry off the body lice, working slowly, carefully depositing the lice in a blue USO envelope. His eyes were tired. It had been a long two weeks in the bush. After an hour or so he sealed up the envelope, wrote FREE in the upper righthand corner, and addressed it to his draft board in Ohio.

On occasions the war was like a Ping-Pong ball. You could put fancy spin on it, you could make it dance.

I remember Norman Bowker and Henry Dobbins playing checkers every evening before dark. It was a ritual for them. They would dig a foxhole and get the board out and play long, silent games as the sky went from pink to purple. The rest of us would sometimes stop by to watch. There was something restful about it, something orderly and reassuring. There were red checkers and black checkers. The playing field was laid out in a strict grid, no tunnels or mountains or jungles. You knew where you stood. You knew the score. The pieces were out on the board, the enemy was visible, you could watch the tactics unfolding into larger strategies. There was a winner and a loser. There were rules.

I'm forty-three years old, and a writer now, and the war has been over for a long while. Much of it is hard to remember. I sit at this typewriter and stare through my words and watch Kiowa sinking into the deep muck of a shit field, or Curt Lemon hanging in pieces from a tree, and as I write about these things, the remembering is turned into a kind of rehappening. Kiowa yells at me. Curt Lemon steps from the shade into bright sunlight, his face brown and shining, and then he soars into a tree. The bad stuff never stops happening: it lives in its own dimension, replaying itself over and over.

But the war wasn't all that way.

Like when Ted Lavender went too heavy on the tranquilizers. "How's the war today?" somebody would say, and Ted Lavender would give a soft, spacey smile and say, "Mellow, man. We got ourselves a nice mellow war today."

And like the time we enlisted an old poppa-san to guide us through the mine fields out on the Batangan Peninsula. The old guy walked with a limp, slow and stooped over, but he knew where the safe spots were and where you had to be careful and where even if you were careful you could end up like popcorn. He had a tightrope walker's feel for the land beneath him—its surface tension, the give and take of things. Each morning we'd form up in a long column, the old poppa-san out front, and for the whole day we'd troop along after him, tracing his footsteps, playing an exact and ruthless game of follow the leader. Rat Kiley made up a rhyme that caught on, and we'd all be chanting it together: *Step out of line, hit a mine; follow the dink, you're in the pink.* All around us, the place was littered with bouncing betties and toe-poppers and booby-trapped artillery rounds, but in those five days on the Batangan Peninsula nobody got hurt. We all came to love the old man.

It was a sad scene when the choppers came to take us away. Jimmy Cross gave the old poppa-san a hug. Mitchell Sanders and Lee Strunk loaded him up with boxes of C rations.

There were actually tears in the old guy's eyes.

"Follow dink," he said to each of us, "you go pink."

If you weren't humping, you were waiting. I remember the monotony. Digging foxholes. Slapping mosquitoes. The sun and the heat and the endless paddies. Even in the deep bush, where you could die any number of ways, the war was nakedly and aggressively boring. But it was a strange boredom. It was boredom with a twist, the kind of boredom that caused stomach disorders. You'd be sitting at the top of a high hill, the flat paddies stretching out below, and the day would be calm and hot and utterly vacant, and you'd feel the boredom dripping inside you like a leaky faucet, except it wasn't water, it was a sort of acid, and with each little droplet you'd feel the stuff eating away at important organs. You'd try to relax. You'd uncurl your fists and let your thoughts go. Well, you'd think, this isn't so bad. And right then you'd hear gunfire behind you and your nuts would fly up into your throat and you'd be squealing pig squeals. That kind of boredom.

I feel guilty sometimes. Forty-three years old and I'm still writing war stories. My daughter Kathleen tells me it's an obsession, that I should write about a little girl who finds a million dollars and spends it all on a Shetland pony.

Here's a quick peace story:

A guy goes AWOL. Shacks up in Danang with a Red Cross nurse. It's a great time—the nurse loves him to death—the guy gets whatever he wants whenever he wants it. The war's over, he thinks. Just nookie and new angles. But then one day he rejoins his unit in the bush. Can't wait to get back into action.

Finally one of his buddies asks what happened with the nurse, why so hot for combat, and the guy says, "All that peace, man, it felt so good it *hurt.* I want to hurt it *back.*"

I remember Mitchell Sanders smiling as he told me that story. Most of it he made up, I'm sure, but even so it gave me a quick truth-goose. Because it's all relative. You're pinned down in some filthy hellhole of a paddy, getting your ass delivered to kingdom come, but then for a few seconds everything goes quiet and you look up and see the sun and a few puffy white clouds, and the immense serenity flashes against your eyeballs—the whole world gets rearranged—and even though you're pinned down by a war, you never felt more at peace.

What sticks in the mind, often, are those odd little fragments that have no beginning and no end:

Norman Bowker lying on his back one night, watching the stars, then whispering to me, "I'll tell you something, O'Brien. If I could have one wish, anything, I'd wish for my dad to write me a letter and say it's okay if I don't win any medals. That's all my old man talks about, nothing else. How he can't wait to see my goddamn medals."

Or Kiowa teaching a rain dance to Rat Kiley and Dave Jensen, the three of them whooping and leaping around barefoot while a bunch of villagers looked on with a mixture of fascination and giggly horror. Afterward, Rat said, "So where's the rain?" and Kiowa said, "The earth is slow, but the buffalo is patient," and Rat thought about it and said, "Yeah, but where's the *rain*?"

Or Ted Lavender adopting an orphan puppy—feeding it from a plastic spoon and carrying it in his rucksack until the day Azar strapped it to a Claymore anti-personnel mine and squeezed the firing device.

The average age in our platoon, I'd guess, was nineteen or twenty, and as a consequence things often took on a curiously playful atmosphere, like a sporting event at some exotic reform school. The competition could be lethal, yet there was a childlike exuberance to it all, lots of pranks and horseplay. Like when Azar blew away Ted Lavender's puppy. "What's everybody so upset about?" Azar said. "I mean, Christ, I'm just a *boy.*"

I remember these things, too.

The damp, fungal scent of an empty body bag.

A quarter moon rising over the nighttime paddies.

Henry Dobbins sitting in the twilight, sewing on his new buck-sergeant stripes, quietly singing "A tisket, a tasket, a green and yellow basket."

A field of elephant grass weighted with wind, bowing under the stir of a helicopter's blades, the grass dark and servile, bending low, but then rising straight again when the chopper went away.

A red clay trail outside the village of My Khe.

A hand grenade.

A slim, dead, dainty young man of about twenty.

Kiowa saying, "No choice, Tim. What else could you do?"

Kiowa saying, "Right?"

Kiowa saying, "Talk to me."

This is one story I've never told before.

Not to anyone.

I remember the man I killed—

His jaw was in his throat, his upper lip and teeth were gone, his one eye was shut, his other eye was a star-shaped hole, his eyebrows were thin and arched like a woman's, his nose was undamaged, there was a slight tear at the lobe of one ear, his clean black hair was swept upwards into a cowlick at the rear of the skull, his forehead was lightly freckled, his fingernails were clean, the skin at his left cheek was peeled back in three ragged strips, his right cheek was smooth and hairless, there was a butterfly on his chin, his neck was open to the spinal cord and the blood there was thick and shiny and it was this wound that had killed him. He lay face-up in the center of the trail, a slim, dead, almost dainty young man. He had bony legs, a narrow waist, long shapely fingers. His chest was sunken and poorly muscled—a scholar, maybe. His wrists were the wrists of a child. He wore a black shirt, black pajama pants, a gray ammunition belt, a gold ring on the third finger of his right hand. His rubber sandals had been blown off. One lay beside him, the other a few meters up the trail. He had been born, maybe, in 1946 in the village of My Khe near the central coastline of Quang Ngai province, where his parents farmed, and where his family had lived for several centuries, and where, during the time of the French, his father and two uncles and many neighbors had joined in the struggle for independence. He was not a Communist. He was a citizen and a soldier. In the village of My Khe, as in all of Quang Ngai, patriotic resistance had the force of tradition, which was partly the force of legend, and from his earliest boyhood the man I killed had listened to stories about the heroic Trung sisters and Tran Hung Dao's famous rout of the Mongols and Le Loi's final victory against the Chinese at Tot Dong. He had been taught that to defend the land was a man's highest duty and highest privilege. He accepted this. It was never open to question. Secretly, though, it also frightened him. He was not a fighter. His health was poor, his body small and frail. He liked books. He wanted someday to be a teacher of mathematics. At night, lying on his mat, he could not picture himself doing the brave things his father had done, or his uncles, or the heroes of the stories. He hoped in his heart that he would never be tested. He hoped the Americans would go away. Soon, he hoped. He kept hoping and hoping, always, even when he was asleep.

"Oh, man, you fuckin' trashed the fucker," Azar said. "You scrambled his sorry self, look at that, you *did*, you laid him out like Shredded fuckin' Wheat."

"Go away," Kiowa said.

"I'm just saying the truth. Like oatmeal."

"Go," Kiowa said.

"Okay, then, I take it back," Azar said. He started to move away, then stopped and said, "Rice Krispies, you know? On the dead test, this particular individual gets A-plus."

Smiling at this, Azar shrugged and walked up the trail toward the village behind the trees.

Kiowa kneeled down.

"Just forget that crud," he said. He opened up his canteen and held it out for a while and then sighed and pulled it away. "No sweat, man. What else could you do?"

Later, Kiowa said, "I'm serious. Nothing *anybody* could do. Come on, Tim, stop staring."

The trail junction was shaded by a row of trees and tall brush. The slim young man lay with his legs in the shade. His jaw was in his throat. His one eye was shut and the other was a star-shaped hole.

Kiowa glanced at the body.

"All right, let me ask a question," he said. "You want to trade places with him? Turn it all upside down—you *want* that? I mean, be honest."

The star-shaped hole was red and yellow. The yellow part seemed to be getting wider, spreading out at the center of the star. The upper lip and gum and teeth were gone. The man's head was cocked at a wrong angle, as if loose at the neck, and the neck was wet with blood.

"Think it over," Kiowa said.

Then later he said, "Tim, it's a *war*. The guy wasn't Heidi—he had a weapon, right? It's a tough thing, for sure, but you got to cut out that staring."

Then he said, "Maybe you better lie down a minute."

Then after a long empty time he said, "Take it slow. Just go wherever the spirit takes you."

The butterfly was making its way along the young man's forehead, which was spotted with small dark freckles. The nose was undamaged. The skin on the right cheek was smooth and fine-grained and hairless. Frail-looking, delicately boned, the young man had never wanted to be a soldier and in his heart had feared that he would perform badly in battle. Even as a boy growing up in the village of My Khe, he had often worried about this. He imagined covering his head and lying in a deep hole and closing his eyes and not moving until the war was over. He had no stomach for violence. He loved mathematics. His eyebrows were thin and arched like a woman's, and at school the boys sometimes teased him about how pretty he was, the arched eyebrows and long shapely fingers, and on the playground they would mimic a woman's walk and make fun of his smooth skin and his love for mathematics. He could not make himself fight them. He often wanted to, but he was afraid, and this increased his shame. If he could not fight little boys, he thought, how could he ever become a soldier and fight the Americans with their airplanes and helicopters and bombs? It did not seem possible. In the presence of his father and uncles he pretended to look forward to doing his patriotic duty, which was also a privilege, but at night he prayed with his mother that the war might end soon. Beyond anything else, he was afraid of disgracing himself, and therefore his family and village. But all he could do, he thought, was wait and pray and try not to grow up too fast.

"Listen to me," Kiowa said. "You feel terrible, I know that."

Then he said, "Okay, maybe I *don't* know."

Along the trail there were small blue flowers shaped like bells. The young man's head was wrenched sideways, not quite facing the flowers, and even in the shade a single blade of sunlight sparkled against the buckle of his ammunition belt. The left cheek was peeled back in three ragged strips. The wounds at his neck had not yet clotted, which made him seem animate even in death, the blood still spreading out across his shirt.

Kiowa shook his head.

There was some silence before he said, "Stop *staring.*"

The young man's fingernails were clean. There was a slight tear at the lobe of one ear, a sprinkling of blood on the forearm. He wore a gold ring on the third finger of his right hand. His chest was sunken and poorly muscled—a scholar, maybe. For years, despite his family's poverty, the man I killed had been determined to continue his education in mathematics. The means for this were arranged, perhaps, through the village liberation cadres, and in 1964 the young man began attending classes at the university in Saigon, where he avoided politics and paid attention to the problems of calculus. He devoted himself to his studies. He spent his nights alone, wrote romantic poems in his journal, took pleasure in the grace and beauty of differential equations. The war, he knew, would finally take him, but for the time being he would not let himself think about it. He had stopped praying; instead, now, he waited. And as he waited, in his final year at the university, he fell in love with a classmate, a girl of seventeen, who one day told him that his wrists were like the wrists of a child, so small and delicate, and who admired his narrow waist and the cowlick that rose up like a bird's tail at the back of his head. She liked his quiet manner; she laughed at his freckles and bony legs. One evening, perhaps, they exchanged gold rings.

Now one eye was a star.

"You okay?" Kiowa said.

The body lay almost entirely in shade. There were gnats at the mouth, little flecks of pollen drifting above the nose. The butterfly was gone. The bleeding had stopped except for the neck wounds.

Kiowa picked up the rubber sandals, clapping off the dirt, then bent down to search the body. There was a pouch of rice, a comb, a fingernail clipper, a few soiled piasters, a snapshot of a young woman standing in front of a parked motorcycle.

Kiowa placed these items in his rucksack along with the gray ammunition belt and rubber sandals.

Then he squatted down.

"I'll tell you the straight truth," he said. "The guy was dead from the second he stepped on the trail. Understand me? We all had him zeroed. A good kill—weapon, ammunition, everything." Tiny beads of sweat glistened at Kiowa's forehead. His eyes moved from the sky to the dead man's body to the knuckles of his own hands. "So listen, you have to pull your shit together. Can't just sit here all day."

Later he said, "Understand?"

Then he said, "Five minutes, Tim. Five more minutes and we're moving out."

The one eye did a funny twinkling trick, red to yellow. The head was wrenched sideways, as if loose at the neck, and the dead young man seemed to be staring at some distant object beyond the bell-shaped flowers along the trail. The blood at the neck had gone to a deep purplish black. Clean fingernails, clean hair—he had been a soldier for only a single day. After his years at the university, the man I killed returned with his new wife to the village of My Khe, where he enlisted as a common rifleman with the 48th Viet Cong Battalion. He knew he would die quickly. He knew he would see a flash of light. He knew he would fall dead and wake up in the stories of his village and people.

Kiowa covered the body with a poncho.

"Hey, Tim, you're looking better," he said. "No doubt about it. All you needed was time—some mental R&R."

Then he said, "Man, I'm sorry."

Then later he said, "Why not talk about it?"

Then he said, "Come on, man, talk."

He was a slim, dead, almost dainty young man of about twenty. He lay with one leg bent beneath him, his jaw in his throat, his face neither expressive nor inexpressive. One eye was shut. The other was a star-shaped hole.

"Talk to me," Kiowa said. **Q**

VOICE
RUN-ONS

Graceland

Because I got out is the reason life picks up when I fly in, and that I bring along some Yankee, it makes them wild, stirs them up. But this time, flying in, something in the air means things more and it is not just my Yankee is worse than the others I have brought along with me at other times, no, I think it is death itself adding the somber note, I felt it reaching its hand up to my airplane as my airplane was glinting in for the touchdown. It was a finger I saw outside my window seat crooking down and I pointed it out to Bradley, who said he could make it out too once I had shown him what I felt.

It is true that only because I am in town Agnes cuts into her crucial praying time and gets up off her knees and stands herself a little taller even though she is sick and is hot and clammy, and some other thing the tests have shown that have got her crazy scared, and she is standing next to me dressed in fuchsia chiffon, and this is how I know it is me that is the reason for these changes, as she is touching me and no one else, weaving her fingers with mine, drumming her nails in my palm, kissing me on the lips and behind the ear. Bradley stays close, is rocking back on his heels, lowering his chin, and seeing out from prescription sunglasses that get light inside and dark outside and is looking over at the mural on the wall done in greens, of Spanish moss and a plantation.

Agnes is wondering about him, and my guess is so is everybody else wondering, and she says to me, "He looks like an Italian count, and you look different too, Justine," she says. I will not discuss me, but I do take the time to tell her no, that Bradley just looks like he looks because he works in a big department store, in the men's department, and gets a discount, is where he buys these wonderful clothes he wears that probably are from Italy, in fact they probably are, I am sure of it, and she nods and twists the ring I am wearing on my finger, it is one of the ones she has sent me in the mail, and I look over at Bradley, and him tall and thin, and I see where Agnes is getting her thinking from, from nowhere other than just from looking with her eyes like any one of us could do.

Me, I will not get into it with her and discuss, as Agnes has her ideas of how I should look to look my best, and this is not it, as I have done myself up in mostly black starting with a black little skinny dress, my hair color now changed to black and my hair ratted out full away from my face, but my lips red as berries is the look I have now, all my own new look except for one thing. I am wearing a lot of big chunky jewelry, all of it what she has been sending me in the mail, all of it hers, like pearls and aquamarine earrings, and thick gold chain brace-lets, and more; there is a giant flower brooch pinned on my dress. I have thought to bring her a present though I do not know when I can find some quiet for her to open it.

We all are waiting a long time to move from the cocktail hour to the big table for dinner, as we are tied up with waiting for certain cousins to arrive, from where they are driving in from the eastern part of the state and they are not too reliable.

But Agnes is, to my mind, becoming more reliable the way she sees things, clear as day she sees things more than just seeing Bradley and noticing my change in dressing style, she sees things close to the way I do I have recently come to know, as we have been writing these letters back and forth since things got even harder in my life, me trying to find someplace to make a life on this planet and her finding out she was soon going to be leaving the planet altogether.

We started out with dashing off little notes and cards back and forth, and her saying she had gone to the doctor before or after her bridge game or ladies' church luncheon and me saying, "Oh, I know how scared you must be because I got back this bad smear from my doctor back here in the East and I am worried half to death," and then her saying, "Come on home, Justine, and let us take care of you," and her sending

me a bracelet, or some cash in the mail, and me writing back
and saying, "Don't worry, Agnes, I had another one and it all
went away, it cleared up, I think it was the carrot juice Bradley
fixed me that did it," and her writing that there is a shadow on
her X-ray, and me saying, "Agnes, you come East where the
real doctors are that will know what to do about that shadow,"
and her saying, no, she would die on the airplane, and finally
she writing me in a different tone altogether and asking me
about did I know what happened after you died, and me writing her back the things I think about that as best I could, me
writing her back plainly because she is clearly desperate with
wanting to know from somebody, and her saying in so many
words she has never been so alone, and so I say I know I would
be scared like her if I was like her, if I was ninety-one years old
and sick, and I tell her just that in my letters. I tell her to keep
praying, that I would, you betch your life. I know I would be
at Lourdes right now if it was me. And I would be too, I would
be in Mexico swallowing apricot pits if it came to that, I would
be rubbing bat grease in my hair if it would help, I would be
hysterical like her, out of my head. And so she has been sending me all her jewelry and even some large bills in the mail to
my little apartment, my little place, and her letters are getting
more bald with the truth of her heart with every one I get, and
so are mine starting to be with the power of telling the truth
as we see it to each other, and it is a dazzling experience, the
most dazzling of my life to now, I tell you, Agnes and I discov-
ering each other.

They circle around us, blood family does, holding drinks.
My Yankee turns from the mural to the window and his glasses
are graceful, they darken up spreading like dye in water just
because he has turned toward a lamp. There is no sun in here.

"Well, I want to speak," Agnes says, "before the cousins
get here even. I just want you all to know that I am glad you
are here, and as I told you already, I would rather see you all
together once more with me alive than for you to come back
to my funeral where I would not know it."

Then somebody says, "What in the Sam Hill funeral are you talking about, Agnes?"

"What funeral, Agnes, you are looking grand, just grand," somebody else says.

"Let us drink a toast to Agnes," a third person says, and everybody is raising his glass and drinking to Agnes, and she looks over at me, and I look over at Bradley, who has got his shades that are black now up on his head with tufts of hair sticking out around the earpieces, and it is at this time that the French doors fling back and it is the cousins, Bubba and Brick, blowing in from the east part of the state late, just arriving.

There are a lot of "Hey, y'alls, how you doings," and Bubba and Brick, in tandem, head to the bar laughing and elbowing each other and talking about how they need a jump start for this old party. Agnes comes over to me and says for me to be nice to them, Justine, so I say I will, and the next thing I know we are seated at the table, and Bradley is down at the head with Agnes, and I am at the other end between Bubba and Brick.

"Like your little bitty skirt, Justine," Bubba says. He is big, with dark hair. "I like women half-naked," he says.

I tell them about the East, and how I am doing with looking for a job.

Then Brick, who is quieter, with tight lips and blond wavy hair, thumbs down the table, referring to Bradley, and what he means is where in the hell did I get him? and Bubba says, "Just what is it he is wearing anyway, some kind of tweedy faggy ensemble, or what?"

This sets them off laughing, and next they upend their drinks and have to do rock, paper, scissors to see who is going to the bar for refills.

I say to Brick, "I read about you all in *Time* magazine."

Brick waves Bubba back from the bar, yelling across the dining room, "Get over here, Bub. Justine's brought up the World's Fair."

They say, boy, they wish that World's Fair would come back, as there are the lawsuits and they could use the money. They say, "I mean, Justine, that World's Fair was some godsend, I never had so much fun as when that thing was going on," and they are both speaking now, one says one thing and the other one says the next.

"We got this tram concession," Bubba says.

"Had those little trams with the awnings," Brick says.

"We got an exclusive," Bubba says.

"And we let the people park free in our 7-Eleven lot," Brick says, and on like that.

"And then we charged them ten dollars to go back and forth on our tram," one of them says.

"Why didn't you all come down, Justine, and have some fun?" the other one says.

Then Brick gets up and goes and gets three more drinks for us, and the dinner keeps on like that, and my stomach is rumbling, and I am hungry, and all I have had is some little tiny Cajun things off a tray a waiter has passed.

I look down the table to where Agnes is sitting and giving me concern, and to where Bradley is who I have brought along so I will be able to wink at him and have him excuse himself and come and talk to me is the plan, maybe put his arm around me and act possessive for five minutes, or go and get me another drink, or maybe even this, tell me, just say to me, Justine, you must stop now, you have had enough to drink and drinking more will not help one thing and I am taking you and tucking you in bed back at the motel out near the airport so we will be ready for our flight out in the morning.

But Bradley is having fun now, or maybe I never made his part of the plan clear, and I see he is pushing back his chair and doing something with his napkin, like snapping it out in front of him, and I see Agnes, see that her head is kind of slumping over, like she is looking at something in her lap, at least that is what I hope she is doing, her hair looks a little off center, and that startles me it is so sad and so pathetic, and I feel tiny needles of panic fire off in my upper arms. I think that I have not done a thing for her yet except wear her jewelry and spend her money on plane tickets for Bradley and me, and I am worried that I will not think of anything to do, that I have done it all by just writing her a few letters, and I know, I know it has not been enough.

Now Bubba and Brick are shut up about the World's Fair and are watching Bradley too.

"Now what is that dumb Yankee doing now, Justine?" they are saying on either side of me, and I see Agnes's head is drooping even lower than before.

There is nowhere safe to look, it all upsets me, every bit of it, so I am looking out the window of the dining room where we are, and I can see snowball bushes heaping up which bring like a formula to mind Agnes's jewelry I am heaped all over with, and parked beside them is maybe what I think it is, my mind does a thing, there cannot be too many of them around. Looking out the window of the private dining room and next to a pink snowball bush is, heavy with metal, holes, big tires, and old, Agnes's car, her old Oldsmobile, no matter how old it gets it is her new car to me, and new-car smell is triggered off in my head and I am not imagining, I am smelling it like it really is.

"Earth to Justine," Brick says.

"Now, look at that dumb Yankee," Bubba says, and my head snaps around off the car, and Bradley is doing origami with his napkin, I swear he is. He is making certain folds with the corners, then laying the whole napkin out on the table and doing a couple of crosswise folds across the middle, then holding it up, bending it all around. The ladies are leaning forward, and even the help is lined up behind his chair watching, and he holds it up about head level, and all of a sudden we all see Bradley has made a dog out of that napkin, even with a little tail on it and floppy ears, and he is tossing it one-handed across the table where there is a scuffle to catch it, and then all the women clap their hands and say, "Bravo, Bradley," but not Bubba, and not Brick, and not me, and not Agnes.

I am trying to think of a way to get Bradley to look at me, as it is time for the motel even if I have not given Agnes her present yet, I can mail it to her, but that is not to be, as then he starts in again on someone else's napkin, and I recognize the folds, he is going to make an airplane, and will throw it down to our end of the table, I know, and he will probably hit me in the head with it, messing my hair, Bradley will.

"You want to see something, Justine?" Brick says, jerking his chair closer to mine. "You watch Bubba here, do it for her, Bub. You just wait, Justine."

Bubba grabs up his napkin in his fist. "I am not going to make some wimpy dachshund, uh-uh," he is saying, and he starts folding his napkin, keeping it deep in his lap the whole time while Bradley did different, Bradley had his right up there where everyone could see it the whole time, but Bubba is doing different.

I start thinking about myself, and about Agnes, and I start thinking one thing, that she may be dying but also, that if I do not get myself out of here, I will be dying right along with her, or before her even, and not have lived sixty of the years that she has on her, I will just have skipped right over them without a trace and be dead before she is, we are in an even race, it feels like, and both of us are going flat-out.

Bubba says, "Now look here, Justine," and he is making more folds in his lap and Brick has his arm thrown on the back of my chair and is crowding me, and I am watching Bubba's lap, and slowly it rises up, a long white napkin point coming slowly up out of his lap, and he says, "There, Justine. Now what do you think of them potatoes?—this here is no dachshund."

That is it, that is all I need, with or without Bradley I am pushing back my chair knocking into a waiter holding a rack of lamb, and I am going on down the table and grabbing Agnes up out of her chair and draping her over my arm, they all think I am taking her to the ladies' room, even Bradley reaches a hand back at me as I walk past his chair and he pats in my direction, and Agnes and I head out some French doors onto the flagstone patio, and tiptoe through some clipped grass in our high heels, step over the parking-lot stones going to the waiting Oldsmobile, Agnes's car, which is not locked and which Agnes has the set of keys to. I say to her, "You are sick, aren't you?" and she says, "I am sick to death, Justine, but I do not want to go home or to the hospital. Maybe I will want to go later but not now."

I get her settled in the front seat, and go on around to get in the driver's side, but not without picking a big heavy bunch of snowball flowers from the snowball bush, all colors I get mixed up in the bouquet, and I lay them down on the seat between us, the front seat is like a love seat or a small couch, and the seat belts just strap across our laps and buckle in the old way.

As I start up the Olds, the engine sounds like it has phlegm in its throat, nothing like any new-car sounds, nothing at all, and I find a big two-lane avenue by the country club with big mansions on each side and get us going down it so Agnes can talk to me about anything, and we have all night is how I see it, as I am not leaving here until the morning. She does not mind the wind blowing her hair, she says, and anyway, I go slow, I have just nowhere to go in a hurry at all, and we roll along, her reaching over to put a stray piece of my black hair back up where it goes, and I reach the back of my hand up to her forehead, then to her cheek to check for a fever, which she has, that I know, and then she does it, she does the thing, she reaches up and instead of straightening her hair she takes it off and drops it on the seat by the flowers between the two of us, and when I look over at her, I see she does have some, just a little bit is all, just thin wisps of it in long thin strands hanging on her head.

"Well, I do not know where to go," Agnes says, "but I want to go somewhere and just sit with you, Justine."

And I say, "Agnes, I have not lived here in a while, but I will try and find us someplace for that."

I think to go and get us a bite, but neither of us wants to eat or go anywhere where there are people we might have to say something to, so I just ride us around, Agnes taking off something from time to time like her watch, and strapping it on my wrist, and then her ring, and slipping it on one of my bare fingers, and next she is taking money from her purse and stuffing it in the side pocket of my purse, and nothing can get her to stop doing these things.

After a long while driving I get an idea, and I turn the car around and head us in the other direction, as now I know where it is that we should be, I head us way over across town through stoplights, and when I tell Agnes where we are going, she says, "Well, Elvis was always kind to his mother," and I guess he was at that, always kind to his mother.

We are at Graceland and Graceland is closed, so Agnes and I just sit out in the Olds in front of the locked gates, which is as close as we can get ourselves, and we wonder to each other for a while if Elvis is dead or not, as there is always that rumor, while a guard saunters around from time to time to check things. Then it comes to me to do something. I grab up the snowball bouquet and slip out of the car and go up close to the fence to see up at the house, but it is hard to see anything much in the dark and there are no lights. My arm with the fewest bracelets is the one I work through the fence bars reaching for some blades of grass from the lawn to have some-thing, and those bracelets Agnes gave me clanking on the metal bars, metal on metal, and this tickles me for some rea-son, me loaded down with things I would not be caught dead in, stealing grass blades at Elvis's, and Bradley back at the country club stuck with my relatives, and Agnes as close to being spirit as possible, and now in my sole care, Agnes looking on. I pull some blades of grass up by the roots, then, standing up, decide to give the snowball bouquet a heave right over the fence here, and with Agnes watching me, I do just that, and they arc up in the sky for a minute and that is the end of them that I can see.

I get back in beside Agnes, and I drop a few little grass blades in her hand, her taking them in her fingers and messing with them as I am digging out the present I have brought her, out from my purse, Agnes saying over and over, "Honey, I do not want anything from you."

She tears the paper and drops the ribbon on top of her wig, and she has my present—in a silver frame, a shot of me, shot so my eyes stand out bleached and lined with black, how I am doing my eyes these days. She says, "Justine, I do not care what you do, or how you get yourself up, or what you try next," and I am feeling a heavy load lifting off my heart.

I start the engine just for the heat now for her, she is shivering, and I say to her, "Agnes, you keep on with your program, Agnes. You are not just anyone to let go and slide down in the mud, you have not lived ninety-one years to do that with yourself."

Then she scares me to death, she says, "Something else, Justine," her breathing in my ear. "Something else, Justine."

I look at her, holding her, but holding her back from me a little, and she says, "I am so scared, I am still scared, and I cannot believe it that I would feel this way by now but I do, it is not any better going into someplace you just do not know, you do not know and cannot see."

I say to her, I say, making a mistake saying it too, I think, I say, "Agnes, you are making me scared with the way you talk about what is ahead because I would expect by now you would know, and be at a kind of peace by now."

Then Agnes starts messing with the grass blades, her hands kind of jerking, and I am more scared than before because I think maybe I just told her to shut up is what she is hearing from me, or that I told her in so many words she should be peaceful, old as she is, and I see next she is putting a piece of that grass between her lips to try something I cannot believe she would know how to do, but she tries to play something on that grass blade, but all she can do is make buzzings, and sharp twerps, and mostly it sounds like air rattling through her lips with no grass harp there at all, and I am wanting her to stop but do not know how to say that to Agnes, so I put the Olds in reverse and back us carefully into the boulevard there in front of Graceland.

I drive us around town like that, Agnes playing never anything really but noises, though once I think maybe I can hear something. After a while I see Agnes drops the grass blades in her lap, just lets them scatter, then she curls her hand over some of them and turns, looking at me.

So I say to her that we have to go now, Agnes, and I head us back across the town. **Q**

New Format

"Can I ask you something?" he said.

"What?" she said.

"Is there something funny going on?" he said. "Down there, I mean."

"Down where?" she said.

"Down there," he said. "In your crotch, I mean. Something, well, wrong or funny. I mean, why is my tongue all numb? Why is that?"

"I don't know," she said. "Maybe you were moving it too fast."

"Was it fast?" he said.

"It was fast," she said. "Hey, I know what that is," she said.

"Oh," he said.

"Spermicide," she said.

"Spermicide?" he said.

"Mm-hm," she said.

"Will all my teeth fall out or something?" he said.

"No," she said, "but all the germs in your mouth will die."

"So that's good," he said.

"Yes," she said, "that's good."

"I knew you were wetter than usual when you came in," he said. "I thought it was me. But it was just the spermicide."

"It was more than just the spermicide," she said. "But a lot of it was the spermicide."

"I thought I was a hot mama," he said.

"You're a hot mama," she said.

"Spermicide," he said, "and a diaphragm, and a prophylactic," he said.

"I'm sorry," she said.

"No, no," he said. "I like the spermicide. I like the diaphragm. I'm not crazy about the prophylactic, but I appreciate it. I'm glad it's there."

"Okay," she said.

"Can we get more up there?" he said. "Can we get a sponge and an IUD and some foam up there too?"

"No," she said. "All we can get is the diaphragm, the spermicide, and you."

"Okay," he said. "I like the diaphragm," he said. "It's like something less mysterious than the crotch itself. Something man-made. It's like having a McDonald's in every city."

"Uh-huh," she said.

Then they didn't say anything.

Then he said, "When I was younger I had this girlfriend. Actually, she wasn't my girlfriend. She was my best friend's girlfriend. My *best friend's.* But she still wanted to do it with me and I still wanted to do it with her. So we would do it."

"Uh-huh," she said.

"But we needed rubbers, and I was too scared to buy them. I was only sixteen."

"Mm-hm," she said.

"So I had her sneak up to his room, my best friend's room, and she would steal rubbers from her boyfriend to do it with me."

"Wow," she said.

"I wanted to have sex," he said.

"I understand," she said. "How's your tongue?"

"Still tingly," he said. "Maybe if you knew I was going to do that, with your crotch, I mean, maybe you could put that stuff in later on."

"How can I know if you're going to do that?" she said.

"I don't know," he said. "I never know what I'm going to do."

"Maybe you should just make sure you do that every night," she said.

"No," he said. "I don't want to do that every night. Maybe on Wednesdays and Fridays."

"What about Saturdays?" she said.

"No," he said. "I won't do it on Saturdays."

"Maybe you should get on the pill too," he said.

"I am on the pill," she said. "Maybe you should get a vasectomy."

"I got a vasectomy," he said.

"Oh," she said. "I used to use this other thing. It was a little tablet. You shove it up there and it dissolves."

"Wow," he said.

"But I only used it once. It said on the side of the box that it might cause a burning sensation."

"Holy cow," he said. "Did it?"

"Not to me," she said. "But him."

"Oh," he said.

"Just one more thing," she said.

"What?" he said.

"It might be a cliché," she said.

"That's okay," he said.

"Hold me," she said.

Then they didn't say anything. **Q**

SUBJECT MATTER
(HIP)

Farted

I was in the Bone Café in Harvard Square, where I eat a muffin and a coffee every morning for breakfast. The place is pretty clean, but I put up with it because I like watching all the people, especially the girls, walk by. Every morning I eat my muffin and coffee by myself and watch people.

Today I was over near the door, watching, eating—there was a pretty Indian girl who was nervous because I kept staring. There was a nervous guy waiting for a date. He was real obvious about it. He walked all around the Bone Café craning his neck, around and around and walked outside of the Bone Café and over to the T stop and then back, craning his neck. There was also a sort of couple sitting in front of me. And I was sort of watching, sort of listening, and I figured they hadn't known each other for very long. They were both being real polite about how they were eating their croissants, and wiping their mouths a lot, and if they had to cough or sniff they did it real timidly.

They were getting to know each other and saying things like: "So what year are you?" and "Where did you grow up?" and then they would just nod very quietly when there were holes in the conversation.

And I farted. Not for any mean reason, just because I had to. And it came up around me for a second and it was pretty stinky, maybe the stinkiest in the world.

Anyway, I could tell by the way the wind was blowing that the fart was headed their way—that it was going to swarm around them for a while, stay there for a little bit before it moved on or disappeared.

And I knew what was happening too. I knew that he was sitting there going—*Oh, God, who farted? Oh, God, what if she thinks I farted?* And she was thinking—*Holy cow, I hope that wasn't him,* and *Oh, God, what if he thinks that's me?* But no matter what, I knew that, forever, they would associate each other with that fart, possibly the stinkiest.

I had been feeling kind of down, insignificant.

But after I farted, I felt a little better. **Q**

Something Like That Song
Fanny Brice Used to Sing

All of Birdie's men are on stakes in the garden—the two housepainters, each with one kitchen-colored leg; the big Marine with the matchbook still in his pocket from a place Birdie knew, some name in Maine; the gendarme with silk socks; the New York City cop; the propane man; and what was left of the Civil War boy with the breast-pocket bullet hole Bible-high—all thrust through the gut with floorboards from the bedroom upstairs too big for Birdie's single bed anyway, their shoulders strutted out with parts of barn or bed slats, the better to be seen, to mark time, to scare crow.

Only the Russian was still alive.

Birdie kept the Russian in the garden anyway on an iron bed that straddled three rows of Harvard beets and a patch of sorrel, volunteered through mulch and snow for schav. The Russian's presence, Birdie thought, would help keep the wilder deer from attacking Birdie's tender young shoots, and provide shade for Birdie's late summer lettuce, there where he stretched the whole Russian winter length of him, stuck as the slugs Birdie captured each night in overturned cabbage leaves and tinny pools of beer, tangled in cobwebs, curing in the sun, while Birdie stood by watching, hoeing row and hilling leek. There would be a sign. Birdie knew this from God. So Birdie parked the Russian's taxi in the barn behind the house and prepared herself for revelation.

Birdie harvested all of Birdie's men and hoisted them high on their crisscrossed boards and bedslats to face the door and to wait for further orders from the Russian. She would visit them there and knit them mittens and scarves, for they would all need new clothes when the Russian redeemed them. She would sit in the taxi with the meter running in case she had soup on or bread in the oven, but mostly she would work in the Russian's garden, worrying his head with warm birch beer, waiting for his fever and her torment to be lifted. There was a moment when the Russian spoke and pulled at Birdie's beets and told Birdie stories that made no sense to Birdie at all: about pallets made of pine branch for dogs to sleep on and how to keep the edge on an iron scythe and cotton harvests in this land he came from, close to China, where men wear turbans and speak Uzbek and grow grapes as big and pink as a big man's big toes, as big and pink, he would say, as the tip of his penis just trimmed by the zealots who had met him at the airport, pale and pious bearded men who have a stake in such things. Birdie bathed his head and then bathed her own in the warm comfrey tea she kept in the sun, but this moment she remembered as speech did not return.

From time to time she would undress him and lift his separate parts the way she might pull a carrot to look for stout, turning a leg one way and then another, smelling an elbow, thumping a head. When the sun was small overhead and his big hand was on the twelve, she would try to feed him—a little mashed banana or some oatmeal and tea. But mostly she listened to his fevered Russian ravings—so many *r*'s she thought, somewhere they understand this—willing the pickle vines to curl around her legs and the legs of the bed that held the Russian, up tendril, curlicueing up through broken bed springs, pickle vines paler in the sleeping shade of him, strong and green and willing as they belted through his loops, climbing under cuff and curving into sleeve and collar, binding the Russian to iron and to Birdie's fertile ground.

The next morning she discovered the Russian standing pissing and she saw what she knew to be the sign from God there where the Russian stood standing and pissing und blue jays that fly here to scream from Massachusetts. T pomegranate. The pomegranate ripe and swollen with s the pomegranate there at the tip of his Russian penis, a b ing forth from him of a fruit of holy dimension, a bulb tha been forced in her garden overnight. Birdie open-thro sound and ran to touch it, ran to taste it, but the Russian, wild-eyed like the wilder deer, ran away, trailing vine of pickle and weed, tripping over brush grass and rapeseed and burdock, buckle-kneed and hot-palmed from the heft of his staggering load, heading away from Birdie and to the barn with Birdie's men . . . God! . . . then letting go a sound that Birdie knew to be only human, then showing to Birdie a face that Birdie had seen many times before.

It was the face of the two house painters with kitchen-colored legs; the big Marine with the matchbook still in his pocket from a place Birdie knew, some name in Maine; the gendarme with silk socks; the New York City cop; the propane man; and what was left of the Civil War boy with the breast-pocket bullet hole Bible-high. So Birdie thrust the Russian through the gut with a floorboard from the bedroom upstairs too big for Birdie's bed anyway, and nailed the Russian's shoulders to a crosspiece made of barn. When the day cooled, she would hoist him up-timber to join the others, but first there was nightsoil to till into the cornrows and trimmings to scatter from last night's carrots, streams to dam, and ponds to skim, and eggs to gather, and trees to name. There was earth to move from here to there. Birdie was half a mind content to just go on going on in her garden. Her work would be done well before dark and then Birdie could sit among the melons and have soup. After all, she thought, this is a perfect place for staking ground, for rocking chair, for watching road. **Q**

DAN LEONE

Mother

I'm sick of hearing about broken hearts and shattered dreams. From now on, I want to see broken arms and shattered kneecaps before I lend anyone my shoulder. You want real pain? Have a baby. Mine came out sideways, my daughter. I made like she was an angel and she grew up and called me an asshole—but that doesn't hurt. What hurts is her pounding out of you like a tractor.

My first husband stabbed me in the stomach. My second husband shot me in the foot and set the house on fire. Believe me, it doesn't hurt one bit that this is what love has come to for you. What hurts is the hole in your skin. That hole has big-league pain inside it, and my daughter's never felt that. She's twenty-something and never had a baby. She's never been shot, stabbed, or burned in a fire.

So what was she carrying on about when I went to see her yesterday?

"What's the matter, honey?" I said.

She was sitting on her bed, wearing just a big brown towel, and she was looking up at me all wet in the face and shrugging her shoulders. The girl's got a nice apartment and a good job. Her boyfriend's studying to be a doctor.

"What is it?" I said.

"I don't know, Ma," she said. "It's nothing. I'm just confused, that's all."

"My God," I said, "what's confusing you?"

She shook her head. Then she started crying again.

"Are you sick?" I said. "Did he punch you?"

I sat down on the bed and she slapped her arms around me and sobbed on my shoulder.

"There, there," I said.

I wanted to help, believe me, but what can you do? And

33

her hair was making my face itch. You've got to understand about this girl, she has beautiful hair. She has everything going for her. The boy, the job, the apartment. Like I said, she's smart and beautiful. I'll tell you what, look at my daughter and you'd never guess she's had anything to do with me, or vice versa. Of course, her father was good-looking, too. But now he's dead. My first husband killed him. Then he stabbed me in the stomach, trying to kill the baby.

But that's where she got her looks—from a dead guy I screwed around with. And ever since my second husband got put away, it's been pretty smooth sailing for the girl. Birthdays and Christmas trees. She has a lot of friends.

That's why I don't understand.

"Did that son-of-a-bitch hit you?" I said.

"Ma, he's the nicest guy in the world," she said. "He doesn't hit me. He wants to marry me." She showed me the beautiful ring he got her. It was beautiful.

I didn't say anything. I just sat there and held her and let her cry.

"I love him, Ma. But I'm so mixed up."

She cried and cried.

I just held on to her, opened up my mouth around the top of her arm, and bit down as hard as I could. She started screaming and tried to pull away, but I had her all wrapped up, spider-style. I clamped down with my teeth until I felt the blood coming out at the corner of my mouth.

This is it, I said to her in my head. I mean, welcome to the world, you know what I mean? **Q**

Freelance Johnson

It's true, sir, that I speak English, but maybe I am not so good for you. Maybe you can ask Captain Habib to assign someone else, and let me tell you why, sir. You understand we have many freelances coming to our war zone for such purposes as in making famous photographs. This is what Freelance Johnson told me, the reason why so many Americans are coming here. And he had a camera just like yours, sir, looking all black with expensive quality. So I tried to help Freelance Johnson because those were my orders from Captain Habib.

First we went to the village of Nijra, there to make pictures of sorrowful women and those childs without arms. These are ignorant people, you will understand, and they began at rock throwing when the camera came upon them. Even I am struck here upon the forehead but still wishing to cooperate when Freelance Johnson puts to me the camera.

"Let the blood come between your fingers" was his instruction.

And I told him, "Sir, maybe we can leave this village now."

Because at that time, you know, a crowd was gathered with much anger for bombs and shellings which made wall removals on their houses. But Freelance Johnson prefers his pictures, until one such rock flew at his camera glass, the same glass as on your camera, sir, and breaking it we came away.

The next day I requested from Captain Habib someone other to proceed with Freelance Johnson, but my English is borne upon me so I did my best. This time Freelance Johnson wishes he will make photographs of the broken airplane near Aram al Shakra.

"Sir," I told him, "if you please, that airplane is too close to enemy positions."

But Freelance Johnson is very brave, so we go there, to

Aram al Shakra, and at that place we receive bullets which placed a chip of rock in my eye. You can see it here, sir, something wrong in this one eye.

Now, still to cooperate, even suffering such pain in my face, I made to wait while Freelance Johnson stood upon the hill to collect pictures of the enemy. Only with my pain I forgot to mention some mine field which guards that place and in the manner of feet positions he explodes himself. It was both legs which came from his body, wearing shorts, sir, with those big pockets just like on your own. So this is my unhappy memory and I think maybe you can ask Captain Habib for some new guide. Just my helpful suggestion, sir. **Q**

The House Itself

A FOUND TRAGEDY

Cast

ERIC—*He works in the house.*

IRIS—*This tall girl has tried to buy new bread.*

HOGAN—*He eats.*

THE OLD MAN—*The old man who arrived yesterday.*

TAD—*The cook's child.*

TOM—*He goes.*

ROSS—*He cultivates.*

GIL—*A man who is wanting work.*

SIMON—*He hasn't even a cent.*

DONNA—*The teacher who hit me.*

BROOKE—*She has gone to town.*

ASHLEY—*The youth who will not return.*

JESSIE—*Skilled person.*

MARIE—*The girl who came.*

CARL—*He has a high opinion of himself.*

DET. CALLAHAN—*A trustworthy stranger.*

Scene 1: THE HOUSE WHICH THEY LIVED IN.

ERIC: *When will the guests arrive?*

IRIS: *Look for the children!*

HOGAN: *The boys aren't playing football today.*

THE OLD MAN: *I have no children.*

TAD: *Give me the thing I want.*

TOM: *The child is bad.*

HOGAN: *This orange tree does not bear well.*

THE OLD MAN: *We have no food.*

ROSS: *The planks are split. The door is undone. Eggs are obtainable in the market.*

IRIS: *Bring bread!*

ERIC: *How shall I open this door?*

IRIS: *Don't open the door! Shut the door!*

HOGAN: *Many people do not eat bread.*

GIL: *Our cattle like eating that sweet grass.*

TOM: *The old man is ill.*

ERIC: *Will he come today?*

TOM: *I don't know, but it is possible.*

HOGAN: *My father does not know how to read.*

THE OLD MAN: *I am ill.*

SIMON: *The town was big. The knife will be sharp.*

ERIC: *How many spoons?*

Scene 2: THE SHOP WHICH HE OPENED.

DONNA: *This shop is very nice.*

BROOKE: *The old man is waiting at home.*

ASHLEY: *This coconut is larger than that one.*

DONNA: *That shop is not very nice.*

BROOKE: *The old man waits at home.*

JESSIE: *If the cat goes away, the rat rules.*

DONNA: *These stones are hard.*

MARIE: *As for me, I don't want to go.*

BROOKE: *The old man has waited at home.*

JESSIE: *He who climbs the ladder comes down.*

DONNA: *These stones are not hard.*

ASHLEY: *These trees are not coconuts.*

MARIE: *I look for a man who can do heavy work.*

Scene 3: AT THE HOUSE.

CARL: *And I said to my wife, "Go and shut the door," and she said to me, "You go and shut it."*

ERIC: *Who are these girls?*

THE OLD MAN: *Our town has not many people.*

ERIC: *What sort of things did they buy in town?*

TOM: *Are you ready?*

ROSS: *The road is impassable.*

ERIC: *How many trees fell down?*

ROSS: *The house is invisible.*

ERIC: *Why has he gone home?*

DET. CALLAHAN: *We have not yet agreed on this matter.*

THE OLD MAN: *These towns have no people.*

ERIC: *What is that animal eating?*

IRIS: *I don't eat chicken.*

HOGAN: *The animal has eaten a child.*

THE OLD MAN: *This cup is not clean.*

TAD: *Give me the thing I want.*

DET. CALLAHAN: *The child has come. The arm is broken.*

ROSS: *Many animals are fierce, but others are not fierce.*

HOGAN: *This thing is no use. Everyone has gone home.*

THE OLD MAN: *This room has no one.*

HOGAN: *In all directions there is rubbish.* **Q**

SETTING

Fires

Some years the heat comes in April. There is always wind in April, but with luck, there is warmth, too. There is usually a drought, so that the fields are dry, and the wind is from the south. Everyone in the valley moves their seedlings from the indoors to the outdoors, into their old barns-turned-into-greenhouses. Root crops are what do best up here. The soil is rich from all the many fires, and potatoes from this valley taste like candy. Carrots pull free of the dark earth and taste like crisp sun. I like to cook with onions. Strawberries do well, too, if they're kept watered.

The snow line has moved up out of the valley by April, up into the woods, and even on up above the woods, disappearing, except for the smallest remote oval patches of it, and the snowshoe hares, gaunt but still white, move down out of the snow as it retreats to get to the gardens' fresh berries and the green growing grasses; but you can see the hares coming a mile away, coming after your berries—hopping through the green-and-gold sun-filled woods, as white and pure as Persian cats, hopping over brown logs, coming down the centuries-old game trails of black earth.

The rabbits come straight for my outside garden like zombies, relentless, and I sit on the back porch and sight in on them. But because they are too beautiful to kill in great numbers, I shoot only one every month or so, just to warn them. I clean the one I shoot and fry it in a skillet with onions and half a piece of bacon.

Sometimes at night I'll get up and look out the window and see the rabbits out in the garden, nibbling at whatever's available, but also standing around the greenhouse, all around it, just *aching* to get in: several of them digging at the earth around it, trying to tunnel in—dirt flying all through the air—

while others of them just sit there at the doorway, waiting.

The hares are only snow-white like that for a few weeks, after the snow is gone; then they begin to lose the white fur—or rather, they do not lose it, but it begins to turn brown, like leaves decaying, so that they are mottled for a while, during the change, but then finally they are completely brown, and safe again, with the snows gone. But for those few weeks when they are still white, the rabbits sit out in my garden like white boulders. I haven't had a woman living with me in a long time now. Whenever one does move in with me, it feels as if I've tricked her, have caught her in a trap: as if the gate has been closed behind her and she doesn't yet realize it. It's very remote up here.

One summer, my friend Tom's sister came up here to spend the summer with Tom and his wife, Nancy, and to train at altitude. Her name was Glenda, and she was a runner from Washington, and that was all she did, was run. Glenda was very good, and she had run in races in Italy, in France, and in Switzerland. She told everyone when she got up here that this was the most beautiful place that she had ever seen, told all these rough loggers and their hard wives this, and we all believed her. Very few of us had ever been anywhere else to be able to question her.

We would all sit out at the picnic tables in front of the saloon, ten or twelve of us at a time, half the town, and watch the river. Ducks and geese, heading back north, stopped in our valley to breed, to build nests, and to raise their young. Ravens, with their wings and backs shining greasy in the sun, were always flying across the valley, from one side of the mountains to the other. Anyone who needed to make a little money could always do so in April by planting seedlings for the Forest Service, and it was always a time of relaxation because of that fact, a time of no tempers, only loose happiness. I did not need much money, in April or in any other month, and I would often sit out at the picnic table with Glenda and Tom and Nancy and drink beer. Glenda would never drink more than two. She had yellow hair that was cut short, and lake-blue eyes, a pale face, and a big grin, not unlike Tom's, that belied her seriousness, though now that she is gone, I think I remember her always being able to grin *because* of her seriousness. I certainly don't understand why it seems that way to me now. Like the rest of us, Glenda had no worries, not in April, and certainly not later on in the summer. She had only to run.

I never saw Glenda in the fall, which was when she left; I don't know if she ever smiled like that when she got back to Washington or not. She was separated from her boyfriend, who lived in California, and she didn't seem to miss him, didn't ever seem to think about him.

The planters burned the slopes they had cut the previous summer and fall, before planting the seedlings, and in the afternoons there would be a sweet-smelling haze that started about halfway up the valley walls and rose into the highest mountains and then spilled over them, moving north into Canada, riding on the south winds. The fires' haze never settled in our valley but would hang just above us, on the days it was there, turning all the sunlight a beautiful, smoky blue and making things when seen across the valley—a barn in another pasture, or a fence line—seem much farther away than they really were. It made things seem softer, too.

There was a long, zippered scar on the inside of Glenda's knee that started just above her ankle and went all the way up inside her leg to mid-thigh. She had injured the knee when she was seventeen, long before the days of arthoscopic surgery, and she'd had to have the knee rebuilt the old-fashioned way, with blades and scissors, but the scar only seemed to make her legs, both of them, look even more beautiful, the part that was not scarred, and even the scar had a graceful curve to it as it ran such a long distance up her leg.

Glenda wore green nylon shorts and a small white shirt when she ran, and a headband. Her running shoes were dirty white, the color of the road dust during the drought.

"I'm thirty-two, and have six or seven more good years of running," she said whenever anyone asked her what her plans were, and why she ran so much, and why she had come to our valley to run. Mostly, it was the men who sat around with us in front of the saloon, watching the river, watching the spring winds, and just being glad with the rest of us that winter was over. I do not think the women liked Glenda very much, except for Nancy.

It was not very well understood in the valley what a great runner Glenda was.

I think it gave Glenda pleasure that it wasn't.

"I would like for you to follow Glenda on the bicycle," Tom said the first time I met her. Tom had invited me over for dinner—Glenda had gotten into the valley the day before, though we had all known that she was coming for weeks beforehand, and we had been waiting for her.

"There's money available from her sponsor to pay you for it," Tom said, handing me some money, or trying to, finally putting it in my shirt pocket. He had been drinking, and seemed as happy as I had seen him in a long time. He called her "Glen" instead of "Glenda" sometimes—and after putting the money in my pocket, he put an arm around Nancy, who looked embarrassed for me, and the other arm around Glenda, who did not, and so I had to keep the money, which was not that much, anyway.

"You just ride along behind her, with a pistol"—Tom had a pistol holstered on his belt, a big pistol, and he took it off and handed it to me—"and you make sure nothing happens to her, the way it did to that Ocherson woman."

The Ocherson woman had been visiting friends and had been walking home, but had never made it: a bear had evidently charged out of the willows along the river road and had dragged her back across the river. It was in the spring when she disappeared, and everyone thought she had run away; and her husband had even gone around all summer making a fool out of himself by talking badly about her, and then hunters found her in the fall, right before the first snow. There were always bear stories in any valley, but we thought ours was the worst, because it was the most recent, and because it had been a woman.

"It'll be good exercise for me," I said to Tom, and then I said to Glenda, "Do you run fast?"

It wasn't a bad job. I was able to keep up with her most of the time, and we started early in the mornings. Some days Glenda would run just a few miles, very fast, and other days it seemed she was going to run forever. There was hardly ever any traffic—not a single car or truck—and I'd daydream as I rode along behind her.

We'd leave the meadows out in front of Tom's place and head up the South Fork road, up into the woods, toward the summit, going past my cabin. The sun would be burning brightly by the time we neared the summit, and we'd be up into the haze from the planting fires, and everything would be foggy and old-looking, as if we had gone back in time—as if we were living in a time when things had really *happened,* when things still mattered and not everything had been decided yet.

Glenda would be sweating so hard from running the summit that her shirt and shorts would be drenched, her hair damp and sticking to the side of her face, and the sweat would wet her socks and even her tennis shoes. But she was always saying that the people she would be racing against would be training even harder than she was.

There were lakes up past the summit and the air was cooler; on the north slopes the lakes still had thin crusts of ice over them, crusts that thawed out, barely, each afternoon, but that froze again each night, and what Glenda liked to do after she'd reached the summit—her face as bright as if sunburned, and her wrists limp and loose, sometimes wavering a little in her stride, finally, so great was the heat, and her exhaustion—was to leave the road and run down the game trail leading to the lakes—tripping, stumbling, running downhill again; and I would have to throw the bike down and hurry after her—and pulling her shirt off, she would run out into the shallows of the first lake, her feet breaking through the thin ice, and then she would sit down in the cold water, like some animal chased there by hounds.

"It feels good," she said, the first time she did that, and she leaned her head back on the ice behind her, the ice she had not broken through, and she spread her arms out across the ice as if she were resting on a crucifix, and she looked up at the haze in the sky, with nothing above us, for we were above the tree line.

"Come over here," she said. "Come feel this."

I waded out into the pond, following her trail through the ice, and sat down next to her.

She took my hand and put it on her chest.

What I felt in there was like nothing I had ever imagined: it was like lifting up the hood of a car that is still running, with all the cables and belts and fan blades still running. I wanted to take my hand away; I wanted to get her to a doctor. I wondered if she was going to die, and if I would be responsible. I wanted to pull my hand away, but she made me keep it there, and gradually the drumming slowed, became steadier, and still she made me keep my hand there, until we could both feel the water's coldness. Then we got out—I had to help her up, because her injured knee was stiff—and we laid our clothes out on rocks to dry in the sun, and we lay out on flat rocks ourselves and let the wind and the sun dry us as well. She said that she had come to the mountains to run because it would strengthen her knee. But there was something that made me believe that that was not the reason, and not the truth, though I cannot tell you what other reason there might have been.

We went into the lake every hot day, after her run, and there was always the thinnest sheet of ice, back in the shadows. It felt wonderful; and lying out in the sun afterward was wonderful, too. After we had dried, our hair smelled like the smoke from the fires in the valley below. Sometimes I thought that Glenda might be dying, and had come here to live her last days, to run in a country of great beauty.

After we were dry, we walked back, and as we went back over the crest of the summit and started down toward the valley, we would slowly come out of the haze, and would be able to see all of the valley below us, green and soft, with the slow wind of the Yaak River crawling through the middle of it, and on the north wall of the valley, midway up the slopes, the ragged fires would be burning, with wavering lines and shifting walls of smoke rising from behind the trees, sheets of smoke rising straight into the sky.

The temptation to get on the bike and just coast all the way down was always strong, but I knew what my job was, we both did, and it was the time when bears were coming out of hibernation, when everything was, and the safety of the winter was not to be confused with the seriousness of summer, with the way things were changing.

Sometimes, walking back, we would come upon ruffed grouse—males—courting and fanning in the middle of the road, spinning and doing their little dance, their throat sacs inflated bright and red, pulsing, and the grouse would not want to let us past—they would stamp their feet and spin in mad little circles, trying to block where it was we were going, trying to protect some certain small area they had staked out for themselves. Glenda seemed to stiffen whenever we came upon the fanning males, and shrieked when they rushed at her ankles, making as if to peck her.

We would stop back by my cabin for lunch, on the way back into the valley. I would open all the windows—the sun would have heated all the logs in the house, so that when we came inside there was a rich dry smell, as it is when you have been away from your house for a long time and first come back—but that smell was always there, in my cabin—and we would sit at the breakfast-room table and look out the window, out at the old weedy chicken house I'd never used but which the people who had lived in the cabin before me had built, and we would look at the woods going up onto the mountain behind the chicken house.

I had planted a few wild apple trees in the back yard that spring, and the place that had sold them to me said that these trees would be able to withstand even the coldest winters, though I was not sure I believed it. They were small trees, and it was supposed to be four years before they began bearing fruit, and that sounded to me like such a long time that I had had to really think about it before buying them. But I just bought them without really knowing why I was doing it. I also didn't know what would make a person run as much as Glenda did. But I liked riding with her, and having coffee with her after the runs, and I knew I would be sad to see her leave the valley. I think that was what kept up the distance between us, a nice distance, just the right-sized distance—the fact that each of us knew that she was only going to be there a certain amount of time—that she would be there for the rest of May and June, and all through July, and on through most of August, but that then she would be gone. We knew what was going to happen, it was a certainty, and therefore it seemed to take away any danger, any wildness. There was a wonderful sense of control. She drank her coffee black. We would snack on smoked whitefish that I had caught the previous winter.

I had a couple of dogs in the back yard, Texas hounds that I'd brought up north with me a few years ago, and I kept them in a pen in the winter so that they wouldn't roam and chase and catch deer, but in the spring and summer the sun felt so thin and good and the hounds were so old that I didn't keep them penned up but instead just let them lie around in the grass, dozing. There was one thing they would chase, though, in the summer. It lived under the chicken house—I don't know what it was; it was dark, and ran too fast for me to ever get a good look at it—and it's also possible that even if I had been able to see it, it would have been some animal that I had never seen before—some rare animal, something from Canada perhaps—maybe something no one had ever seen. Whatever it was—small and dark, with fur, but not shaggy, not a bear cub—it never grew from year to year, but always stayed the same, though it seemed young somehow, as if it might *someday* grow—anyway, it lived in a burrow under the chicken house, and it excited the dogs terribly. It would come ripping out of the woods, just a fleet dark blur through the woods, headed for the burrow, and the old dogs would be up and baying, right on its tail, but the thing always made it into the burrow just ahead of them.

Glenda and I would sit at the window and watch for it. But it kept no timetable, and there was no telling when it would come, or even if it would. We called it a hedgehog, because that was the closest thing we figured it resembled.

Some nights Glenda would call me on the shortwave radio, would key the mike a few times to make it crackle and wake me up, and then, mysteriously, I would hear her voice in the night, floating in static, as if it were in the night, out with the stars—her voice: "Have you seen the hedgehog?" she would ask, sleepily, but it would only be a radio that was in the dark house with me, not her, not her real voice. "Did you see the hedge-hog?" she'd want to know, and I'd wish she were staying with me, I'd wish she were with me at that moment. But it would be no good—Glenda was leaving in August, or September at the latest.

"No," I'd say. "No hedgehog today. Maybe it's gone away," I'd say—though I had thought that again and again, dozens of times, but then I would always see it again, just when I thought I never would.

"How are the dogs?" she'd ask. "How are Homer and Ann?"

"They're asleep."

"Good night," she'd say.

"Good night," I would say.

On Thursday nights, I would always have Tom and Nancy and Glenda over for dinner. Friday was Glenda's day off from running, so that she could drink, could stay up late, and she did not have to worry about any aftereffects the next morning. We would start out drinking at the Dirty Shame, sitting out front watching the river, watching the ducks and geese headed north, and then before dusk we would go back down to my ranch, and Glenda and I would fix dinner while Tom and Nancy sat on the front porch and smoked cigars and watched the elk come out into the dusk in the meadow across the road.

"Where's this famous hedgehog?" Tom would bellow, blowing smoke rings into the night, big, perfect O's, and the elk would lift their heads, chewing the summer grass like cattle, the bulls' antlers glowing with velvet.

"In the back yard," Glenda would say, washing the salad, or rinsing off the carrots, or the trout filets. "But you can only see him in the daytime."

"Aww, *bullshit*!" Tom would roar, standing up with his bottle of Jack Daniel's, and he'd take off down the steps, stumbling, and we'd all put down what we were doing and get flashlights and go with him to make sure he was all right, because Tom was a trapper, and it riled him to think there was an animal he did not know, could not trap, could not even see—Tom had tried to trap the hedgehog before but had never caught anything—and Tom did not believe there was any such animal. Out by the chicken coop, Tom would get down on his hands and knees, breathing hard, and we'd crowd all around and try to shine the flashlight into the deep, dusty hole, to see if there might be a patch of fur, the tip of a snout, *anything*—and Tom would be making grunting noises that were, I supposed, designed to make the animal want to come out—but we never saw anything, and it would be cold under

all the stars, and we'd be able to see the far-off glows that were
the planting fires, burning slowly, even into the night, but
which were being held in check by backfires; they were in
control.

We had one of those propane fish fryers, and we'd put
it out on the front porch and cut the trout into cubes, roll them
around in sweet mustard and flour, then drop them in the hot
spattering grease. We'd fix more than a hundred of the trout
cubes, and there were never any left over. Glenda had a tre-
mendous appetite, eating almost as many as would Tom, and
licking her fingers afterward, asking if there were any more.
We'd take whatever we were drinking up on the roof—Tom,
his Jack Daniel's, and Glenda and I, rum-and-Cokes, and
Nancy, vodka—and we'd sit high on the steep roof of my cabin,
above the second-story bedroom dormer—Tom sat out on the
end of the dormer as if it were a saddle—and Glenda would
sit next to me for warmth, as we'd watch the far-off fires of the
burns, a flaming orange color as they sawed their way across
the mountainside, raging, but contained. Below us, in the back
yard, those rabbits that had still not turned brown would begin
to come out of the woods, dozens of them, moving in on the
greenhouse and then stopping, just lining up all around it,
wanting to get into the tender young carrots and the Simpson
lettuce. I had put sheets down on the ground out in the back
yard to trick them, and we'd laugh as the rabbits moved ner-
vously from sheet to sheet, several of them huddling together
on one sheet at a time, thinking they were protected; and, all
the time, moving in on the greenhouse.

"Turn back, you bastards!" Tom would shout happily,
whenever he saw the rabbits start coming out of the woods in
the moonlight, and his shouts would wake the ducks down on
the pond, and they would begin clucking to themselves, quack-
ing, and it was a reassuring sound. Nancy made Tom tie a rope
around his waist and tie the other end around the chimney in

case he fell. But Tom said that he wasn't afraid of anything, and that he was going to live forever.

Glenda weighed herself before and after each run. I had to remember that I did not want to grow too close to her, as she would be leaving. I only wanted to be her friend. We ran and rode in silence. We never saw any bears. But she was frightened of them, even as the summer went on without us seeing any, and so I always carried the pistol. We had been pale from the long sunless winter, but were beginning to grow brown from lying out by the lake up at the summit. Glenda took long naps after her runs, we both did, Glenda sleeping on my couch, and I'd cover her with a blanket and lie down on the floor next to her, and the sun would pour in through the windows, and there was no world outside our valley. But I could feel my heart pounding.

It turned drier than ever in August. The loggers were cutting again. It was always dry and windy, and the fields and meadows turned to crisp hay. Everyone was terrified of sparks, especially the old people, because they'd seen the big fires rush through the valley in the past, moving through like an army—the big fire in 1901, and then the monstrous one, in 1921, that burned up every tree except for the very luckiest ones, so that for years afterward the entire valley was barren and scorched, smoldering—and the wind in our faces was hot, and we went down to the saloon in the early afternoons, after we had stopped off at my cabin, and we'd drink beer.

Glenda would lie on her back on top of the picnic table and look up at the clouds. She would be going back to Washington in three weeks, and then down to California, she said. We were both as brown as nuts. Almost all the men would be off in the woods, logging. We would have the whole valley to ourselves. Tom and Nancy had been calling us "the lovebirds" in July, trying to get something going, I think, but they stopped in

August. She was running harder than ever, really improving, so that I was having trouble keeping up with her near the top of the summit, on the days that Glenda ran it.

There was no ice left anywhere, no snow, not even in the darkest, coolest parts of the forest, but the lakes and ponds and creeks and rivers were still ice-cold when we leaped into them, hot and heart-hammering; and each time, Glenda made me put my hand on her breast, her heart thumping and jumping around as if about to burst out, until I could finally feel it calming, and then almost stopping, as the lake's cold waters worked on her.

"Don't you ever leave this place, Joe Barry," she'd say to me as she watched the clouds. "You've got it really good here, Joe Barry."

I'd be stroking her knee with my fingers, running them along the inside scar, and the wind would be moving her hair around. She would close her eyes after a while, and it was hot, but there would be goose bumps on her legs, on her arms.

"No, ma'am, I wouldn't do that," I'd say, and take another swig of beer. "Wild horses couldn't take me away from this place—no, they couldn't."

I'd think about her heart, jumping and flapping around in her small chest like a fish in a footlocker, after those long runs; at the top of the summit, I'd wonder how anything could ever be so *alive.*

The afternoon that she set fire to the field across the road from my cabin was a still day, windless, and I guess that Glenda thought it was safe, that it would just be a grass fire and would do no harm—and she was right, though I did not know that. I saw her standing out in the middle of the field, lighting matches, bending down and cupping her hands until a small blaze appeared at her feet. Then she came running across the field toward my cabin.

I loved to watch her run. I did not know why she had set the fire, and I was very afraid that it might cross the road and

burn up my hay barn, even my cabin—but I was not as frightened as I might have been. It was the day before Glenda was
going to leave, and mostly I was just delighted to see her.

She came running up the steps, pounded on my door, and
then came inside, breathless, having run a dead sprint all the
way. The fire was spreading fast, even without a wind, because
the grass was so dry, and red-winged blackbirds were leaping
up out of the grass ahead of it, and I could see marsh rabbits
and mice scurrying across the road, coming into my yard. An
elk bounded across the meadow. There was a lot of smoke. It
was late in the afternoon, not quite dusk, but soon would be,
and Glenda was pulling me by the hand, taking me back outside and down the steps, back out toward the fire, toward the
pond on the far side of the field. It was a large pond, large
enough to protect us, I hoped, and we ran hard across the
field, with a new wind suddenly picking up, a wind made from
the flames, and we got to the pond and kicked our shoes off,
pulled off our shirts and jeans, and splashed out into the water,
and waited for the flames to get to us and then work their way
around us.

It was just a grass fire. But the heat was intense as it rushed
toward us, blasting our faces with the hot winds.

It was terrifying.

We ducked our heads under the water to cool our drying
faces, and splashed water on each other's shoulders. Birds
were flying past us, and grasshoppers, and small mice were
diving into the pond with us, where hungry trout were rising
and snapping at them, swallowing them like corn. It was growing dark and there were flames all around us. We could only
wait to see if the grass was going to burn itself up as the fire
swept past.

"Please, love," Glenda was saying, and I did not understand at first that she was speaking to me. "Please."

We had moved out into the deepest part of the pond,
chest-deep, and kept having to duck beneath the surface because of the heat. Our lips and faces were blistering. Pieces of

ash were floating down on the water like snow. It was not until nightfall that the flames died down, just a few orange ones flickering here and there. But all the rest of the small field was black and smoldering, and still too hot for someone with no shoes to walk across.

It was cold. I was colder than I had ever been. We held on to each other all night, holding each other tightly, because we were shivering. I thought about luck, about chance. I thought about fears, all the different ones, and the things that could make a person run. She left at daylight, would not let me drive her home, but trotted, instead, heading up the road to Tom's.

That was two years ago. The rabbits have changed, and then changed again: twice.

The hedgehog—I have never seen it again. After all these years, it has left. I wish I knew for sure that was what it had been; I wish I had a name for it.

Will it be back? I do not think so. Why was it here in the first place? I do not know.

Just the tame, predictable ways of rabbits—that is all I have left now.

Is Glenda still running? It is mid-February. It hurts to remember her. The field across the road lies scorched and black, hidden beneath a cover of snow. **Q**

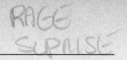

Fried Chicken

I don't know if, in the back of my mind (yeah, I figure my mind is a *place*), I was planning on doing it this way all along. People have a way of doing things, little things maybe, that show how they really feel about you, underneath all the smiles. "And Jim here, Jim would like a drumstick, isn't that right?" said Carl, and I didn't like it one bit. I didn't want no drumstick. That's for kids. I wanted a breast, or a thigh.

Carl was smiling. Yeah, I saw that smile, his wet lips pulled back so I could see his big sharp yellow teeth, teeth that, if he thought he could get away with it, would gnaw me down to the bone. He and old Bob were pretty brave now, in the kitchen, drinking bourbon while Carl's wife fried up something to eat. It was a different story, I'm telling you, back at the bank. Now I could see them looking at each other, secret, like maybe they'd already come up with a way to cheat on the count.

Numbers, you see, man, have a kind of life of their own. And when you get into division, it's like, well . . . Divided by *three,* divided by *four* . . . that's a whole lot different than divided by *one.* There's a lot of sense in divided by *one.* That's what I was thinking, and maybe I'd been thinking it all along. If I didn't trust them, they could probably see it, and then they didn't trust *me,* and that's no good, you can't leave things like that, drive everybody nuts.

Carl's wife, Suzanne, stayed over by the stove. She didn't want to look at me, I could tell. It was hot, and there were a couple of flies in, past the hole in the screen door, and I was sweating, smelling the dirty smell of all that chicken grease, and I was afraid if I got greasy fingers I'd never get anything done. I took a bite of potato salad and said, "This is some fine potato salad, Suzanne."

Carl and Bob both laughed, and it was that laughing—I

55

don't know what was so funny—made it real easy to pull my second gun, a .32, out from my armpit under the leather jacket they'd said something about me wearing in the heat.

"Hey, kid . . ." began Carl—he was always talking, always had an expert opinion on everything—then, right after I shot him in the face, Suzanne swung the skillet of hot grease, so I shot her and then Bob, who'd caught himself most of the chicken fat and was making some kind of noise. I shot him dead.

Twice in the heart.

Shit, I could always shoot.

I was all jacked up, and Suzanne didn't seem too bad. She had an old butcher knife and just about nailed me. She tried to stick it in me and just nicked me through the leather jacket as I put the last few bullets into her and jumped away. I was trying to keep from stepping in a lot of blood. I never had anything against Suzanne. She made a sandwich for me once when I came over and no one else was home. But what was I supposed to do? She knew there was nothing left to talk over, no way I could leave her be.

I got what I needed, some weaponry, the money, and some other stuff, like hitting the medicine cabinet just in case, and I walked out of that house, chewing on a piece of chicken—a breast, in case you're interested—that so far as I was concerned needed some salt. I wasn't about to go back inside after a saltshaker, though, you can bet. It still tasted pretty good.

Divided by one. That's me. **Q**

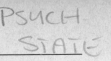

JAN PENDLETON

Inside the Roomer's Room

I wanted to be the roomer who came to our house and rented the roomer's room. I wanted to be the ever-so-tidy roomer who put his things in the drawers and closets inside the roomer's room, the man who took his things from a suitcase and put his clothes, the very same clothes that were folded up inside his suitcase, put them inside the drawers and closets that were inside the roomer's room. I wanted to be the man who rocked back and forth in the black wicker chair that was inside the roomer's room, have my breakfast brought to me on a tray. I would only go out of the room to visit the library, and I would come back with a stack of books to put on my dresser. Maybe I would have a cat, and the cat would sleep on the afghan that was folded across the foot of the roomer's bed.

Sitting up on a stool that was in the middle of the roomer's room, I watched my mother cleaning up after the roomer who had moved away, getting ready for the new roomer to move in. My mother swept things from under the bed into a giant dustball in the middle of the room. "I don't know how you can just sit and watch people work," my mother said. I could smell the minty smell of my mother's Stinger, which was beside me on the stool.

Women moved into the roomer's room with their babies, and sometimes the babies had sour, gone-off milk in their bottles with crusted-shut nipples from where the old, sour milk had dried and stuck together. The women dated Navy men from Moffett Field. Some of the women got pregnant and had abortions, and they lay on our living-room couch with their gray, women's faces, filling the house with the smell of their bleeding. I could hear the sound of the women's babies being scraped away, first the babies' eyes, then the babies' arms. Then the entire rest of the babies. I could hear this and the

57

sound of my father walking around and around our house, his brown man's shoes making a sound on the gravel that was underneath our windows. "Don't worry," my mother would say. "It's just your father trying to take you away." Around and around our house my father would walk, looking inside the windows for the thing that belonged to him.

One night, a man came into our house and handled the things that were sitting out on our tables and chairs, handled the things as if he were handling the people inside our house. I could hear the man picking things up and putting them back down again. I jumped out of the window and cut my feet, and I dripped blood down the circular driveway that was in front of our house, the driveway that was the reason my mother and father bought the house that my mother and I now lived in, the house that had the roomer's room in it, and that my mother and father bought so they could drive their car up one side and down the other side of the circular driveway that was in front of our house.

In the mornings, my mother sat at the breakfast nook with her Stinger. She still had on her black dancing dress and her see-through plastic dancing shoes, and she looked out the window at the gnarled and bent old-women trees with their crab-apple breasts. It would start to rain and my mother would say that the rain was really the old women crying because they did not have babies to suck on their breasts.

Outside, I heard the sound of my father walking around our house with his brown man's shoes, on top of the gravel that was underneath our windows, walking around and around our house like a bear that was looking for food. **Q**

Carnival

The woman has lost her diamond earrings inside the red case the woman carries them in. The woman left the red case with the earrings inside in the bathroom when the bus stopped for lunch. The woman goes to the front of the bus and she tells the driver that she has lost her earrings. The woman has to say it several times before the driver understands the French the woman remembers learning in high school.

The driver's French is fast and it sounds like hard metal keys striking against something. The driver tells the woman to stay on the bus, that he will call the restaurant from Peronne, from the transportation office in Peronne. The driver says that someone in the restaurant will have taken the woman's diamond earrings, that the person will have thrown the woman's earring case inside the toilet. The next driver will bring the case to the woman in Peronne. The woman does not understand why the driver wants to retrieve her earring case.

In Peronne, tourists stare at the woman as if they are waiting for her to do something strange at any moment, stick out her tongue and take off her clothes. The clerk refuses to let the woman use the phone. The driver takes the woman's hand and he leads her to the manager's office, where he phones the restaurant. No one has turned in the woman's red earring case. The driver buys sandwiches and coffee, and he drives the woman back to Paris to the police, where the woman reports what has happened.

When the woman has finished talking to the police, the driver takes her back to the bus and he drives the woman through the city. It is raining and the streets are black. The woman is the only person riding inside the bus, and she sees the driver watching her in his mirror.

The driver takes the woman to his hotel. The woman holds on to the driver, as if the driver is a car that the woman is riding in at a carnival. When the woman closes her eyes, it seems to her that the car she is riding in has thrown itself off the tracks, and that the car is speeding through the air and will crash into something—perhaps into the people who are standing under them, watching. **Q**

SETTING
SUPRISE

Jackpot

I owe a lot to Tim Britten. He hired me to drive him
all over the desert to search for mustangs. He wanted one dead
or alive, he was so eager for a catch. Live ones are better, of
course, but he didn't know the first thing about keeping animals. Neither did I. "You're my cowboy," he'd say, lifting one
of my hands off the steering wheel. I've got big hands. "Grip's
important," Tim said the first time we met. He stood there
hanging on to my handshake like he was about to arm wrestle
and yank me over, so I pulled a little my way and he smiled.
I smiled back. Then his wife, Marlene, said, "Let me see," and
Tim Britten handed me over, so I gripped her hand too. All
of us had big hands. "You must work hard," she said.

The truth is, I'd been working hard on the slots for a few
months, I had the fever so bad. It was just after I'd been fired
for dealing lousy in Reno because I couldn't remember all the
cards. Dealing twenty-one from two decks all night wore me
out. So I played blind, not counting cards, and I lost lots of the
casino's money. It's always *their* money, no matter whose
pocket it comes from. I almost swung work at other houses
until I got blackballed for dicking with one of the coin-toss
machines in Harrah's—I was shoving it, trying to topple silver
into the twenty-dollar hole. The security guards took me to a
back office and I thought they were going to punch me some,
but they only snapped my photo and sent it all over town. They
could have arrested me, but I wasn't worth it, they said. So I
went east across the state, playing little casinos. I wasn't in the
mood for work and I figured if I found trouble I'd head to
Vegas where the casinos wouldn't ride me, they've got so many
big-timers to worry about.

I wasn't eating right and I started drinking a little, mostly screwdrivers, because they're hard to ruin, and before I knew it I was crazy for the slots. It was looking at all those coins— especially dollars and halves—that got me, those machines swollen with silver. And I was winning. It's the worst bet in the casino, any amateur can tell you, but when you're winning at slots, there's nothing like it, because it's a real private thing, just you and the machine, and you can play as fast or as slow as you please. I'd work as many as four machines at a time, all night, until my hands were black from the coins and my fingers nearly numb and my shoulders hot with pain. But you can only keep a streak for a short spell. I slipped until I was playing nothing but nickels. By the time I saw Tim Britten's ad in the Elko *Courier*, I was down to one cardboard bucket of them— about thirty-six dollars—and I knew I had to get away for a while to cool off and dry out.

Tim asked no questions and I suspected I was the only one who'd answered his ad. He wasn't offering any money, just room and board and some shares in his horse ranch, which wasn't built yet. All he had was a trailer on cinder blocks about fifty miles south of Elko—we passed through Carlin, went over the first range, took a turn onto a dirt road, then I was lost. There was a black rocky range to one side and one far off to the other side that had a white streak across the middle, which Tim said was salt. Otherwise, there wasn't anything except waist-high weeds, sage mostly, and long stretches of dirt that rose and fell all around. I had met Tim in front of Aces High in Elko, after waiting around until the top of my head was itchy from sunburn. "You've got an intelligent look," Tim told me. "Doesn't he, Marlene?" "It's the glasses," she said, "they magnify his eyes." I was still wearing my casino outfit—white shirt and black pants with black shoes, what all casino workers wear, except mine hadn't been washed in weeks.

When we got to the "ranch," as Tim called it, he gave me a cowboy hat and some new blue jeans that were too tight and cowboy boots that were too big, and I began that day, driving straight across the desert, doing all kinds of damage to the plant life. Tim would always wear his sunglasses, well-pressed jeans, some long-sleeve cowboy shirt with snap pearl buttons, and a light-colored cowboy hat (seven gallons, he said). He was tall and slump-shouldered and seemed to have spent most of his life indoors, he was so pale. He had shadows under his eyes as if from lack of sleep, and it's true, he slept little, maybe a few hours at a time. He spent most of his nights sitting in a lawn chair out back behind the trailer with a rifle and a bag of potato chips and a flashlight as big as a club. The first few nights, I didn't know what he was up to, so I went out finally and asked him, long after Marlene had gone to bed, "What're you doing, Tim?" He grinned at me. "Waiting for the unexpected," he said.

"Isn't driving like this illegal in the desert?" I asked him in the beginning. The truck rattled over ruts and swayed, the shocks squeaking, as I steered up one slope and down another. The air was always chalky with dust.

Tim kept looking from side to side like he was afraid of missing something or like maybe we were being followed by state troopers or poachers, or I don't know what. "Great thing about Nevada is you don't have to worry about things like that," he said finally. "Look at this." He held out one hand like he was offering me everything I could see. "It's wide open," he said.

The truth is, driving like that across the desert was illegal—there were signs just off the main road that said so. And I'd seen something on the news a year ago that said chasing wild horses was illegal too. But these weren't the first illegal things I'd done.

There wasn't much to it except boredom. The desert stretched on and on and Tim Britten usually said nothing, his rifle aimed out the window. I would have asked him to drive some, only he couldn't. He had trouble coordinating the gas and the clutch, and he never watched where he was going, so he'd veer off, gunning the truck into a ditch or racing headlong into a butte. It was queer behavior for a mechanical genius, I thought. That's what he was, he said, a mechanical genius. An engineer, he said. Just the year before, he'd been helping an oil company look for deposits near Tonopah. That was the first he'd seen Nevada, because until then he'd spent most of his life in school. He was real book-smart. And he had a lot of ideas for inventions—the trailer was crowded with his drawings—but he didn't do anything with them. Besides some pressure-sensitive liquid sensor he'd made for the oil company, the only other Tim Britten invention that ever got completed, as far as I know, was fifty gallons of Even-Steven, an alcoholic drink distilled from pine nuts and non-fat dry milk.

Drinking Even-Stevens was how Tim and Marlene spent most of their time together. They'd drink until they got real quiet and sleepy, then they'd lie next to each other in a lawn chair and lick each other's hands. That's all they did. Lick, lick, lick. It made me prickly to watch them, so I tried to stay out of the way. But that wasn't easy, since the trailer was small and I wasn't about to go out walking, on account of the rattlers all around. Outside, there was nowhere to go, anyway, and nothing to look at except the ridge in the distance, and no shade except next to the silver propane tank at the side of the trailer. So I'd sit on the front steps, fanning myself with the hat Tim had given me. Sometimes Marlene's retarded collie, Frank, joined me, though I wasn't too fond of his company. He'd lick my hand every time I reached down to pet him. Then I'd get prickly again, thinking of Marlene and Tim. That's when I'd ask myself why I was staying on. But I had to admit that, despite the inconveniences—or because of them—I was losing the urge to gamble.

Marlene didn't join me and Tim on the hunt until Frank disappeared. She claimed the poachers had gotten him.

"What poachers?" I asked. They both smiled at me like I was stupid. Tim said, "You've heard of poachers, Lawrence. They're people—" "Marauders," Marlene corrected. "Exactly," said Tim, "they're marauders who are always looking for a steal." Marlene shaded her eyes with one hand and scouted the distance. "They got Frank," she said. "Good old Frank," said Tim. I couldn't imagine why anybody would want Frank. But I didn't say so, because Marlene was sensitive and kind of nervous, always halfway between laughing and crying—you never knew how she'd take an opinion. The truth is, though, Frank was an ugly thing, an overweight collie with a too narrow face and crossed eyes, his coat dusty and knotted and smelling like piss. He was always gagging whenever he ate because he ate too fast, like he was afraid someone was about to take his bowl away. And he couldn't bark. He could make a whispered grunt, but he couldn't bark, no matter how much Marlene coached him. "Talk to me," she'd say. "Tell me what's on your mind, Frank." Frank would look up at her like he was about to cry, his tongue dangling and his whiskers twitching. Then he'd jerk with effort, but all you'd hear would be a grunt. Marlene had had Frank for fifteen years and that was all she could make him do, but she didn't seem to mind. "He's like a brother," she said. I'd always see Frank lying under Marlene's lawn chair while she sunbathed out back.

Sunbathing was what Marlene did most of the time. She had a great tan, wearing bikinis to show it off, though I don't think Tim cared one way or the other. She and Tim had met in Tonopah at the Money Bucket, where Marlene was waitressing. She was in her forties and he wasn't out of his twenties. Marlene had been married once before to a gypsum miner. But he had died after falling down an unfenced mine shaft. They're all over the desert—shaft holes about five feet square. Because of all the brush you won't see them until you're right at the edge. Marlene said she was still in mourning when she met Tim. "But I couldn't stand to see him carried off by the rednecks he was working with," she said. "He was different, you could tell right off. Sensitive. Look at those little gray eyes." I did and Tim grinned at me. "So I stole him that night," Marlene said. I saw her wink at Tim. She said, "He told me about the wild horses he'd seen while scouting for oil, and that was that—we figured wild-horse ranching was for us, because we could be our own bosses and get the animals for free." "And acreage out here goes for next to nothing," Tim added. They had used Marlene's insurance money to buy the trailer (used) and lots of supplies, like canned hams and blocks of cheese food. "It's been like a vacation," Marlene said, "except for dealing with the chemical toilet."

When Marlene joined us on the hunt, she sat in a lawn chair that Tim had bolted to the flatbed. I would've got sick sprawled in the sun like that and jounced around all day long. But Marlene didn't seem to mind. She wanted to find Frank. Tim decided to make a long trip that would last overnight. He was real excited about it and took charge of loading the truck, while I ran errands for him. All I could think about was having to sleep with rattlers around and tarantulas crawling out of holes at night to creep like hairy hands across my face.

We started out the same old way, heading south, early in the morning when it was still cool and the sun was white behind some high clouds. The air was sweet with the smell of sage, but as the day went on and the sun burned through, all I could smell was dust and truck exhaust. This is what I call low desert, because as far as you can see there's nothing growing higher than human height. No cactus or anything like that. Every once in a while you'll see a tree in the dimple of some distant mountain. But those are rare.

We'd been driving for an hour or so when Tim yelled, "Stop! Stop!" I stamped on the brakes. Billows of dust overtook us and it was minutes before I could see what he was excited about. "That's a hoofprint," he said, hopping out of the truck. There was only one print, preserved in the hardened mud. "A pretty sight," Marlene said, placing her big brown hand over it. "It gives me chills—" She stood abruptly, half crying. Then she laughed. "This is so exciting!" she said. Tim wanted to dig it up as a souvenir, so he got out a pickax and took a swing, but he missed and shattered the print. "I don't know much about the desert," I said, "but seems to me that print could've been there for years." Tim was looking down at Marlene as she picked up the pieces of the print like they were a broken plate. "Where there's one, there's hundreds," he said. "It's just a matter of probability." That made me think of gambling and I started wondering if I'd taken a bigger risk than I'd realized coming out here with these two.

By the time we stopped for lunch, Tim was in the mood to shoot something. He said he didn't feel right if he didn't fire the rifle at least once a day. I watched Marlene spread a picnic blanket in the shade of a sandstone cliff, while Tim aimed his rifle at objects on the horizon, where everything was watery with ripples of heat. "Blam blam blam!" he said. Marlene said, "Here, take this," handing me a cheese sandwich, then one to Tim, but he wouldn't take it. Maybe it bothered him to see us eating cheap, because the money was getting low. They'd spent most of Marlene's money on propane and gasoline to keep things running.

Tim decided he'd shoot one of the swallows that were darting to and from their nests in the shade of the cliff. "They probably taste like squab," he said, aiming. I told him there wasn't enough meat on those little birds to feed a cat. He shrugged. "Anything's better than cheese." For a while I watched the rifle barrel stir the air as Tim followed the birds. Then I sat in the truck cab and looked at the map, though there was nothing to look at—no roads, no settlements, nothing much but open country, dry, dusty, and so hot the air seemed to buzz with meanness.

The report of Tim's rifle sounded like the pop of a paper

bag. The recoil kicked him onto the blanket, where he rolled over a bag of potato chips Marlene was eating. "Look what you've done," she said, pushing him off the crushed chips. He got up and looked around for his kill, but the swallows were gone. "Here," Marlene told him, "put some chips on your sandwich—it tastes better that way."

Tim and Marlene usually started drinking Even-Stevens at lunchtime. Tim had brought several one-gallon thermoses of the stuff, tossing each drink down with a paper cup. I didn't drink any, mainly because it tasted awful, kind of like bourbon and buttermilk. But Tim and Marlene drank the stuff cup after cup. They didn't usually start licking each other until dinnertime. "I miss Frank," Marlene said. Her chin quivered.

"Good old Frank," said Tim, pouring himself another Even-Steven.

The sun was almost directly overhead, stealing shade from the cliff. Marlene stretched out on the lawn chair in the back of the truck. I told her too much sun would ruin her skin.

"Do me a favor," she said. "Get me a drink." She wore little white cups over her eyes. A small pool of oil and sweat glistened in her navel.

"I'm going to make an airplane," said Tim, suddenly standing and emptying his paper cup. "A little one. I'll strap a camera to it and send it scouting ahead. It'll save a hell of a lot of gas."

"Does that mean we don't have much left?" I asked. We had two cans tied to the truck, but I hadn't checked what was left at the trailer.

"What would be really great is a video camera on the plane—everything remote control. Then we'd watch the thing over cocktails and crackers. Sound good?"

"You know how to live, Tim." Marlene smiled, her eyes still cupped. Her skin was gleaming.

"Before you work on any more stuff," I said, "you really ought to have the truck repaired." The clutch was chattering and the valves clacking like rocks in a can. "Did you bring the tool box?"

Tim shrugged and took another drink.

"It's dangerous being out here without tools," I said.

"We'll improvise," he said. "Like pioneers."

While Marlene and Tim finished one of the thermoses of Even-Steven, I counted the sagebrushes as far as I could see, pretending they were horses. Then I made bets with myself about how my count would change when I tried again. The numbers were never the same.

A few hours later, we stopped in a dry creekbed, a good place to camp, said Tim. He scanned the horizon with his rifle scope, then the binoculars. "Nothing moving but the heat," he said finally. A vulture circled in the distance, but Tim couldn't make out what had died. "Not big enough to be a horse." The truck ticked as if about to explode. I pissed on the hood, expecting it to sizzle, but it only steamed. Marlene was sleeping, slack-jawed.

"Is she all right?" I asked. "She looks awful oversunned."

"She loves it," said Tim. He poured himself another Even-Steven and sat in the shade of the truck.

I strung up the tarp and told Tim to wake Marlene so she could get some shade. He shook her. The sun cups fell from her eyes and she lolled her head back and forth, like she was drunk. "Ease up," she muttered. Tim patted her cheek. He said, "Come over here and lie down, Marlene." With his help she stumbled off the truck, then took off her bikini top and sat there like an old Indian, her breasts limp and withered. Tim offered her an Even-Steven, but she didn't seem to see it. "Dots," she said. "Goddamn dots all over the place."

"Too much sun," I said.

Tim wanted to scout around before sunset, so we left Marlene and hiked up a steep mound nearby. All was quiet except for the scratch of lizards scrambling over rocks. The sun was low, long shadows streaming from brush and boulders. A quarter mile away, the vulture sat hunkered over the dead animal. Tim took a couple of shots at it, but missed, and the bird lifted off with slow steady wing beats. Tim wanted to examine the dead animal, so we worked our way down, careful not to step where rattlers hide. What we found was a dog, or what might have been a dog. Ants and vultures had done their work on it and little was left but bones and bits of hair. It could have been a collie, but I didn't think it had Frank's colors. Tim knelt like a hunter reading clues. "No signs of foul play," he said, poking the remains with his rifle barrel. "It could have been a coyote," I said. Tim stood up and squinted at the sun. "I wouldn't mind bagging a coyote."

"They're just little dogs," I said. "You wouldn't want to shoot a little dog, Tim."

"I'd shoot Lassie if I had to, Lawrence. This is survival we're talking about."

"We have provisions."

"Cheese?"

"And bread and potato chips."

"What we need is meat. Pork chops and T-bones. That kind of thing. Or maybe rattlesnake."

"I like cheese just fine, Tim."

"They taste like chicken, you know," Tim said.

"I can live on cheese just fine, thanks," I said.

Tim said, "You're not talking like a cowboy, Lawrence." He started flipping over flat rocks with his rifle barrel. "Let's shoot a couple of rattlers and cook them on a spit like shish kebab."

"I don't want shish kebab," I said.

He kicked over a slab of rock the size of a place mat. "Here's one." He crouched for a better view. "Sleeping soundly. Coiled like a piece of garden hose." It was a rattler three feet long and as fat as a toothpaste tube.

I said, "Leave it alone, Tim."

Tim said, "Watch this guy's expression when I wake him."

"Don't," I said.

Tim prodded the snake with the barrel. The snake jerked its head back and was flicking its tongue, its rattles rattling. Tim pulled the rifle trigger but nothing happened. He pulled again. "Wait a minute," he said, like he was asking somebody to stop talking. He'd forgotten to reload. The snake hissed. "Just a minute." The rattler hit Tim's boot. Tim jumped back and the snake hit him again. I was so light-headed from fear I fell back into a clump of thistle. I saw Tim swing his rifle like a bat. Then he reloaded and shot the snake twice, sand and snake bits flying in all directions. "I think that did it," he said. After he had his breath back, he tied the two biggest snake pieces to his belt, where they dangled, oozing blood.

When we got back to camp, it was dark and Marlene was gone. I lit a lantern while Tim poured himself another Even-Steven. "Probably gone for a walk," he said.

"The desert's no place for a walk at night."

"Probably just taking a leak," Tim said.

I called out for her. She didn't answer. Tim started cleaning the snake, chopping and flailing with his bowie knife until his hands were covered with scales and guts. He was pounding the thing with the knife handle.

I sat on the tailgate of the pickup and watched the sky. It was a clear moonless night. I could smell the smell of suntan lotion from Marlene's vacant lawn chair. Tim didn't decide to go looking for her until he gave up cleaning the snake. We called and called, but she didn't answer. Tim swept the beam of his flashlight all around and to our surprise Marlene had been standing nearby the whole time, naked and silent, with a funny smile on her face.

"Hi, Marlene. You see what we got?" Tim held up the battered rattler.

"She's not looking too well," I said.

"How do you feel, Marlene?" Tim took off his hat like he was about to introduce himself.

"Could be sun poisoning or dehydration," I said.

"You hungry?" Tim asked her.

"She's out of sorts, Tim," I said.

"This is not like her," Tim said. "She's probably sick."

"Maybe we should get her to relax," I said.

"You want to relax, Marlene?" Tim said. He started walking to her and she started backing away. "It's me —Tim. Marlene?" Then he went for her and she took off, running.

Tim and I followed in the pickup, Tim bringing along the rifle because, he said, "you never know what's out there."

I'd never seen anyone run like Marlene. She was hurdling shrubs and rocks like a deer. We lost her finally because the truck couldn't make speed in the sand. I scanned a circle with the headlights, but Marlene was gone, so we stopped to listen. Tim opened another thermos of Even-Steven and this time drank straight from it.

"I should've winged her," he said, "just to slow her down a little."

"Shoot her?" I said.

"Just a nick." He pinched together a thumb and forefinger. "This much maybe," Tim said.

"You don't want to shoot your wife," I said.

He took another drink. "I never knew she could run like that," he said. He drank some more. "She's out there, creeping around," he said. "Turn on the lights."

I switched on the headlights and there, not twenty feet from the truck, was a mule—black, gaunt, weather-beaten animal probably half stupid with hunger. It was startled to see us. Tim screamed, "A wild horse!" He propped the rifle on the dash as if to shoot through the windshield. "You ever see ears so big?"

The mule snorted, showing its dark teeth.

I said, "It's a mule, Tim."

Tim said, "Where's your lasso, Lawrence?"

I got a rope from the back of the truck. I'd never thrown a lasso in my life, but I promised Tim I'd give it a try if the mule would stand still for it. I tried and tried and missed each try, while Tim groaned and squirmed. "Come on, cowboy," Tim kept saying. The mule stood there staring like it had never seen people before. Maybe it hadn't. I got the rope around its neck finally after a lot of tosses.

"Hold him!" Tim screamed, jumping in his excitement. "Don't let go!" Tim tied one end of the rope around his waist. "We've got him now!" Tim screamed. He yanked the rope. The mule grew frantic, bucking until the rope was cutting my hands. "Hold tight, cowboy!" Tim screamed. I wanted to tell him to shut up, but I was hurting too bad. I could see that I had all my problems tugging at the end of that rope. So I let go. Tim screamed, "Hey!" and that was the last I saw of him. The mule dragged him off. A while later, somewhere out there, I heard a "Whoa!" but soon it was quiet except for the breeze that was stirring the sagebrush. I waited around for the longest time, but nobody came back. So I ate two cheese sandwiches, then fell asleep on Marlene's chair, the whole thing smelling like flowers because of her.

In the morning, I went back to the trailer, which I had some trouble finding. Frank was there, trotting around like he'd been only out for a walk. He's still an ugly dog and he still gags when he eats, but he's not bad company. He sits under the lawn chair while I take the sun every day. Sometimes I share a thermos of Even-Steven with him. Then I get up to take potshots at lizards, and Frank trots out ahead of me to grunt at noises I can't hear. That's about all we do nowadays. We've got enough supplies to last us for a while, so

I'm looking at this as a vacation, a kind of jackpot I never thought I'd hit.

"Look at that," I say to Frank, waving a hand like I'm offering him the desert. The dog blinks at me and grunts.

I grunt back, letting him lick my hand. **Q**

The Dress

I can walk and talk. I'm having what my mother would call a good day. She has taken me for what she hopes will be a miracle cure. She has taken me out shopping.

I stand in the front of the store, looking out. The world is flat, pressed into itself, layer on layer of buildings and people sprayed with a light that fixes them in place. Like a postcard the world lies in front of me, apart from me. I am walking through it only to get to the other side.

"Are you all right?" my mother asks.

She is going through racks of clothing, touching each piece, laying her hands on the fabric, on one of each dress in every size, as if she can draw magic out of cloth. She is looking for something to prove everything is not slipping out from under. We are shopping in the wrong place.

I am evaporating, disappearing by inches, small increments, so little at a time that no one seems to notice. There is the strange sensation of a slow erasure.

"Is there anything you like?" my mother asks.

I don't really know what she's getting at, but to keep it simple, I point to a blue linen dress.

"If I were going to wear a dress, I'd wear this one."

"It's beautiful," my mother says.

I look at the dress and imagine being buried in it.

It's not what I want.

"Try it on," my mother says.

I shake my head. I imagine being broken into pieces and the pieces being put into soft padded boxes, until the moment when microsurgeons gather to put me back together. Humpty-Dumpty.

My mother is waving the dress in front of my eyes. She is

hypnotically waving the dress in front of me. Here and gone. Here and gone.

"Try it on," she says. "Try it on."

"Why don't you find something for yourself?" I say.

She looks at me for a minute, then she hands me the blue dress. "Here's your dress," she says, pressing it into my arms.

She picks out skirts and blouses and goes into a dressing room. I sit just outside the changing room, waiting with the blue dress folded over on my lap. I close my eyes.

From what seems like far away I hear the rustle of my mother changing. The soft hiss of a zipper up and down, the swish of a slip, and a whispering sound as something rubs against her pantyhose. In these sounds there is the quiet memory of being a child, a witness. Romance and sadness.

I sit on a folding chair, dying, waiting.

The curtain scrapes open, and my eyes open. My mother appears in a black skirt with a black short-sleeve blouse. The fabric does not shine. It pulls in light, sucking it from my heart, holding it there in the darkness of the pleats. From out of the flat black sleeve, her arms are big and fluffy. My mother is pale and tired. I see she is dying as she watches me, and that I am dying for her.

"What do you think?" my mother asks. I look at her. All dressed in black, black, black.

"I don't like it."

"Why?" She looks in the mirror.

I am helping my mother buy the dress to wear to my funeral.

"It's too much," I say.

"Do you want to go home?" she says.

I shake my head.

I don't want to go home. I never want to go home again. I think of home, of going home, of getting into the car and slowly driving through the city, pulling into the driveway and seeing the day's mail waiting in the mailbox. I think of going into the house and, once through that door, feeling exhausted, as though death had taken me for a moment and then brought me back. I feel caught in this, a constant traveling.

"Are you all right?" my mother says.

She asks me this every ten minutes.

I'm dying; she knows that. Am I all right?

"What do you want me to do?" my mother asks. "What can I do?"

I am alone. No matter how close anyone gets, I am alone. I look at her, and for a moment I'm not sure who she is. I am not sure where I know her from. She is still in black, standing in front of three mirrors, turning in circles, watching herself turning. She is turning on her toes.

I am dying of something there is no name for. There are no parts of my body that can be gouged out and then pulled back together in a deep pucker with marionette string. Because it is a disease that has no name, people think it can't kill. My Uncle Harry is a pharmacist, which he thinks makes him a doctor. He says if you can't name it, you can't have it, and that if you can't have it, then you can't die from it.

I am weaker every day.

"Why don't you try the dress on?" my mother asks. "I won't buy it unless you try it on."

"I don't want it," I say.

I wish I were blue. If I were blue, I wouldn't be dying.

"You don't have to buy it if you don't like it; just try it on, for me."

My mother picks the dress up from my lap. She holds it in front of her, high in the air, her arm extended. I am amazed at her strength. I go into a dressing room.

"Do you need help?" she calls.

I shake my head.

She hangs the dress on a hook and pulls the curtain closed. I look for a chair. There is none. I lean against the wall and pull my sweater off. My arms ache. The sweater falls to the floor. I know she can see it on the floor under the curtain.

"You dropped your sweater."

I think of picking it up, think I will pick it up, but am unable to move.

My mother's hand creeps under the curtain and pulls the sweater out.

"I've got your sweater," she says. "I'll hold it for you."

I'm wearing a gray cotton turtleneck. I hold the bottom edge in both hands and pull up. The cotton is thick and warm from my body. I pull up and, as I pull, I am looking at myself in the mirror. I see my body is shrinking into itself, like a grape becoming a raisin. I am so white that I am see-through. I pull the turtleneck over my breasts. For a moment I am a statue.

"Are you all right in there?" my mother calls out.

"Yes."

I look into the mirror one last time. I bend my head slightly and continue to pull on the turtleneck. I am sucked into the darkness of the cotton, blind. I breathe through the fabric. Air comes slowly and feels thin. I pull and I feel my arms failing. I twist and I turn, and when I breathe again, there is no air. The darkness gets blacker. I cough.

"Are you all right?" my mother calls.

I want to scream, but I cannot open my mouth. I am pulling and pulling on the turtleneck. I am coughing through the cloth. I am spinning in great circles.

"Baby?" my mother calls. From far away I hear the curtain open. I feel my mother grabbing at the cloth. She pulls the shirt up and off my head. I fall into my mother's arms.

"I thought I was going to die," I say. **Q**

CRAIG CURTIS

The Man in the Glass Case

When Simon McDavitt turned twenty, he left Brooklyn and took a train to Davenport, behind the Appalachian Mountains, and built a house there, with an iron weathervane and a porch, and two tiny windows below the roof which let light into the attic; and, after five years, after harvest, he bought a brass bed, and he married.

The bride was thin. She had gray eyes, a longish nose, and a beautiful mouth; and, without undue delay, gave him a daughter. The child had eyes that had a different cast to them at different times of day. Five years later, this wife gave McDavitt a second daughter, whose eyes were plain and who had a foot that was wrong.

This was his family.

He tried farming. Mornings and evenings, sometimes in darkness, McDavitt washed his hands at the tap by the barn. Sundays, he took his family to church in a carriage with a folding top. The Bible McDavitt carried with him to church was in two pieces; the back of it was broken, and the loose binding threads were tucked in the gap separating leather and spine. He did not buy a new one. On Saturday evenings, McDavitt read from it, careful to follow the syllabic divisions of names.

In the ninth year of the marriage, McDavitt's wife died in childbirth. Child and mother were buried together, in a sparse ceremony of few words. McDavitt removed his hat, ushered the children back into the house, opened the Bible a second time, and read from it. The daughters sat bolt upright, in chairs of matching wood. They stared straight ahead of themselves—as though the significance of the words lay hidden among the polished angles of knotted wood.

McDavitt brought in a housekeeper, and went back to his plow.

At thirty-eight, he was conscripted into the Union Army and fought, and was wounded once—but not before he saw Gettysburg, and one Confederate general, at less than forty yards, mounted on a horse, among other mounted officers in a forest of birch trees. When Simon McDavitt returned to Davenport and the land about it—and had walked the mile and a half of road that led from the rail line—he arrived one week and a day ahead of his letters, and a week and two days after his second daughter—the child with the wrong foot—died of measles, in a rash of bright spots. McDavitt took the Bible down, read from it—through the clean and combed hair of a new beard—and covered it with a cloth taken from the closet. His girl with the changing eyes stood beside him. She was eleven and a half.

McDavitt dismissed the housekeeper, nailed the shed shut, and the barn, and put wire around the gatepost circling everything he owned, and—with baggage: three bags, one small and two large—took his daughter and got back on a train; and took it—this time much farther—to Billings, Montana, where he opened a store with the proceeds from the sale of his property: a general store and curio shop.

Billings was a scattering of dwellings enclosing a business district that could be walked in the time it took to smoke a cigar halfway down. A general store was needed. But a curio shop was something else—something people in Billings scratched their heads about.

The general store was built first. The finished shelves filled quickly with provisions, with utensils, tools of various kinds. There was a widened shelf for hats. Dust—from flour bags—settled on light and dark brims alike. What was bought at the general store could be bought anywhere—if a person was willing to ride enough for saddle sores. What the curio shop had could be found nowhere else. Everything was strange. And, if not strange, at least historical. Why an ex-farmer who gave up his plow would build and stock such a place no one knew.

Simon McDavitt was careful, saved, managed things piti-lessly. The only luxury allowed was the ordering of dresses for his daughter—whose name was Melanie; and whose singing, at church Sundays, pleased everyone but the Kearney boy, who was deaf.

As the girl grew, she spent more time in the curio shop, wandering about, dusting things—tabletops, glass cases—while McDavitt sat on his stool, at the register of the store, within earshot always. The girl became lovely, far lovelier than her mother had been, the single photograph of whom stood in a frame on the writing table McDavitt did sums on. Her hair, suddenly, was a radiant red-brown. The brows above her eyes were long and faultless.

McDavitt was quick to act. His eyes gazed over the edge of the till with the tenacity of talons. He scanned the various faces looking into hands and pockets, counting out what they owed. Ultimately, he settled on a clerk of twenty-two, whose hands, both of them, were preternaturally small, almost femi-nine, though speckled with patches of fine blond hair, which were repeated in the mustache he kept waxed at both ends, giving to the smooth face a parody of age otherwise absent. It was a plain countenance, utterly without wrinkling.

The young man was willing. There were already stories—even then—of money, mistrustfully and penuriously hidden under floorboards in the curio shop. McDavitt—to the chagrin of the bank managers in Billings—did not deposit his profits. He sequestered them. Where, no one knew.

It did not take many haircuts—the barbershop was a pool of public knowledge—for word to spread; or for the young man—once summoned—to appear at the door of the McDavitt house wearing a new pair of boots McDavitt himself had given change for. The boots, like the face, were wrinkleless.

In August of that year, hardly after the courting had begun in earnest, an Irishman—a drummer and drifter—found his way into Billings, took his bowler hat off, to ward the horseflies from his somewhat lax, characterless head; and, a week later, was gone again, along with the girl and one suitcase. A letter, a single page, was left behind, which Simon McDavitt did not waste his time reading—since the clerk he had in mind for his daughter had already told him, holding a wet cloth to his swollen jaw.

McDavitt—farmer, and prosperous retailer—was now free of all ties. He need no longer concern himself with either marrying women off or burying them. The future belonged to him. The general store and curio shop were successes far beyond his expectations. Within a score of years, it was no longer a curio shop; it was a museum, as the hinged sign declared.

The items McDavitt displayed, in glass cases and on shelves, included wood, stone, metal, and flesh. They made his reputation, over the years—each of which passed as though stolen from him. Occasionally, he mused on that day his daughter had left. All in all, he considered himself well served. He concentrated on business.

There was always something new. There was a strut from one of the new gliding machines. There was a club foot in formaldehyde. There was a fan, under glass, which had belonged to a European opera diva, who submitted to a concertizing tour of the West and Northwest and then fled to Europe. There was a tiny, carved Buddha, in white stone, weathered to yellow perfection. Whenever a new item was entered into the inventory, word spread—beginning at the barbershop. People found they needed something at the general store. Buckboards began arriving, in rain even. On dry days, the dust could be seen from miles around, funneling and drifting. Simon charged an entrance fee. People paid it. People would not wait to see what rumor and expansion had enlarged to the level of the fantastic. They stood in line to squeeze into the sanctuary that bore the odor, perpetually, of dry wicks, ravaged cotton.

Eventually, McDavitt condescended to the necessity of paying a clerk. He brought in a boy to mind the till and the shelves in the general store, and to superintend the museum, be certain all who entered paid. A string of boys followed, as those who preceded them outgrew the pitiful stipend McDavitt was willing to pay. One by one, the boys who had been clerks— who dusted and stocked—left McDavitt and the memory of his boots, took wives, sired children.

One day, Simon McDavitt woke to find he had lived eighty years. His hair had thinned. It seemed to vanish, year by year, about forehead and crown, until every trace of it had abandoned the veined pate, leaving lintlike apparitions, ghosts of hairs indistinct as snow. His nostrils, however, were knotted with fibers; long, bunching filaments, thicker than bristles on a brush. His eyes took on the faded clarity of photographs bleached by sun; the irises washed out. The flesh about them resembled stony rivers of confused skin. The general store and museum were no exception: rafters, windowsills, doors splintered. The pickled foot, suspended weightlessly and tragically in its narrow jar, wrinkled, curled into itself. The floor creaked. Edges of hidden paint could be seen under the succession of fresh coats applied to the sign. McDavitt's hands came to look like gloves. But the collection—for all its aging and familiar items—had grown, and continued to grow, into the talk of the county, since Montana was now a state and had been for years.

McDavitt dealt with people as he always had: he was terse, to the point. Anyone foolish enough to ask whether he had either sons or daughters got the answer quick enough, like something hammered: yes, he had had them; females, two; and a wife, an additional female; and no, they were dead, buried,

out of mind, out of sight. Stories about him carried as far as
the Dakotas: talk about gold and hidden money and mothballs.
There was always someone—a paying customer—tapping,
probing the floorboards, who invariably went to Ford's afterward and—over corn whiskey or sour mash—claimed he had
found it, stepped on it, felt the pressure of all that coinage
welling up under the varnished wood.

"It's got to be in a steel box," some insisted. "McDavitt
wouldn't put it in anything but steel."

"It'll burn, then," others said. "There won't be anything
left but the box. It'll burn, all right, like a torch. Body won't
be laid out fifteen minutes before it burns—whole damn place.
Then someone will get lucky, if he likes touching hot steel."

When the train halted, in a racket of wheezing smoke
and steam, when the final rasp of metal had hushed, she
stepped off, ahead of her bags, and—holding her black dress
up—minced her way to the boardwalk. Those who took notice
said she looked startled. She was anything but beautiful. Her
bags contained the letters. When people heard, they said
Simon McDavitt was mad—that the only thing he could have
done was lie about his age, or simply, foolishly, *fail* to mention
it, in all that bundled correspondence. Billings had to know,
because someone had to marry them.

That first afternoon she waited like a tree, her bags around
her like stones. The shadows on one side of them—and on one
side of her—lengthened, until a carriage pulled up, blocking
the light, and a freckled boy in a white hat helped her with each
article of luggage, and took the reins in hand, and they were
off—woman, boy, and mare; pulling, and being pulled. She
looked decisively Eastern—qualities difficult to enumerate,
but which anyone in Billings, or anywhere in Montana, could
tell at a glance. And she was homely.

What would an eighty-year-old man do with a woman,
even an ugly one, who was not over thirty, if that? Had McDa-

vitt promised her that fortune there, under those boards? Could any reasonably young woman put up with such a present for such a future?

The general store and museum continued to open and close at the usual time, the doors were locked when lamps had been lit in the houses lining the street; the hexagonal brass knob—polished to spidery lines of scrubbing and thumbnailing—was tested, to see it would not budge, according to McDavitt's instruction.

There was a signed marriage license. The names appeared, side by side, in black ink. There were witnesses. When it was done, the minister congratulated the pair, bowing his head slightly to the side, as though wedging a fiddle between chin and chest. The bride shook hands with McDavitt; the smallish curve of pale flesh fell inside the veined claw.

The coldness of autumn settled in, a speckled fire of discolored and discoloring leaves, which crackled under heel. Mornings, people saw their own breath in the air. There was talk, as might be expected; speculation.

"No way in hell," some of the men said.

The town of Billings was delighted, all in all. There was general unanimity. Smiles spread infectiously.

It was the following spring, in fact, late spring; not long before June made the countryside feverish with Indian paintbrush. She was swollen enough for two people; her whole body looked sore. McDavitt said nothing. No one said anything to him. Even visitors to the museum, from other parts, knew enough to keep their mouths shut. McDavitt's eyes flickered like snake tongues behind the black dignity of his clothing, the wry mess of his beard. He collected his fees, directed his clerk about the store, inventoried, supervised repairs, while Billings talked.

"That something inside her will come out dead," they

said—once they got used to the idea that something *was* coming from the woman, and, most likely, was McDavitt's doing. "It'll come out dead as a shot goose."

"If it's alive, it'll have a tail on its behind."

The talk didn't quit.

Mary Gerling's husband was dead. Her sons were married. She was known for two things: midwifery and sewing. "They're about the same thing," she said. "It's all a matter of closing things up, finishing with them." The morning McDavitt's bride went into labor, the boy was sent in the carriage. It was nearly ten months to the day. Within the hour, she was there, inside the house, wiping sweat from the woman's temples and talking to her, as one would talk to a suffering animal. McDavitt remained in the store, counting and then recounting the kerosene lamps shipped to him without an accurate bill of lading; arguing with a drummer over a belt buckle the man claimed was a personal effect of George Armstrong Custer. No cries came through the walls or through the window. The single wail was heard over the crack of the till drawer opening. The boys—twins—spilled into the world with charcoal hair, into the hands of Mrs. Gerling, who washed them, bundled them in calico, and laid them in the arms of their mother.

Mrs. Gerling was paid in coin, taken back in the carriage; and anything anyone knew about the event in question came from her, since she liked talking as much as she did delivering babies. Mrs. Gerling was accordingly precise about the rooms and the furniture in them. She left nothing out. She said it was the *spiritual longing* of this woman that had made it happen. Mrs. Gerling said how thin and pale the woman's blood was.

They grew insatiably. They prospered. Twins. And perfect. Which was a wonder. First, because they lived. Second, because they weren't deformed. Third, because they failed to resemble either of the pair that had made them.

But they were loud. They were quiet only when they closed their eyes. They clenched their fists, shook them, ranted at everything that came near—at the room for *containing* them; at the sunrise, for intruding through the windowpanes. Even so, the mother adored them.

They kept getting bigger. The details of their birth began to fade from Mrs. Gerling's mind. No one was interested anymore—and there had been other births.

Their mother brought them keys, latch keys, door keys, on rings. She denied them nothing. The old man watched through the window, at his ledger, light from the yard rippling over his features. His face betrayed nothing. They belonged to him. They were his. There was a mother to care for them. When they were five, they could be seen, in overalls two sizes too big, scratching with charred wood on rocks and boulders behind the house, carving lopsided, scraggy circles, their hair long and nearly black, curling over the napes of their necks.

Did McDavitt see the flowers, in their pottered vase, on the supper table? The woman picked them on the hill beyond the house; put them in water, after cutting the stems; took them out again, when the petals shrank, when the green leaves turned; took them out with the supper leavings. In the mornings, she could be seen, among grasses on the slope, picking more of the fresh, bright blooms.

It was said he would live to be a hundred—and anything that got in his way would be paid to get *out* of his way. As the boys became six, and then seven, Simon McDavitt began to shrink. What remained of the hair about his head became little more than a halo, scudding down to his tortoise neck. His hands no longer held coins steady. And the woman? People wondered whether she even knew how to count, let alone manage a store. As for outside help, *who,* among those who called Billings a place to live, would not rifle every damn thing McDavitt had, if left to their own designs? It had been taken from them—inch by inch and year by year—until a quarter of the wealth of the town lay hidden between the four sets of planks forming the four walls, multiplied by three. Not even the pickled foot would be spared. Someone would feed it to his neighbor's hogs.

McDavitt had stopped coming to the store. He stayed inside the house. He no longer sat on the porch; head and chest could be seen from the road, surrounded by the leather of the huge chair. There was not a soul who would not willingly help to bury him. There was not an ax which did not keen for those floorboards. And these children, they were not like other children. Neither wife nor brood set foot in the church. McDavitt gave no explanation.

It was spring again. Beyond the roads and fences, people were planting. Precipitation came in swift clouds, passing over the rutted, irregular paths, their middles brimming with unruly grass. The rains were warm. Draining over the earth, they made clear streams, cascades of molten silver. Rivers ran over their banks, flooding fields, and felled trees carried down, clogging makeshift bridges, against which shoes and blankets and sacks caught—to rot in summer, when the rivers went flat again. In the meadows trout settled over their shadows. Things would slow, begin to slow, as spring exhausted itself and slipped into the lull of summer—and then autumn. The air was rife with mosquito, with lightning bug. It was a fact: spring. The silhouette appeared in the window. People said the curtains were a shroud. Everyone in Billings was busy at work. The town carpenter, for instance. His shed was a maze of empty pegs where tools had hung. He already had the pieces cut for it, the wood planks for a box of some kind.

"Coffin," they said. Because that's what they thought it was.

The carpenter had said a *box*.

And that was all he would say.

And what was the glass for? A huge plate of glass. Everyone saw it. Word passed. There was a crowd at the station before it was half unloaded. What was it for? Not one window anywhere had been broken. Did a single corpse need such preparation?

His woman, too, seemed to get more grotesque with each passing day. She hung out her wash, holding pins in her mouth, while the twins played—the profile of McDavitt painted in the window behind them. Even this day she was seen at her wash, at the lines pulling in wind, catching the loosened sleeves, leggings torn from their pins, and smiling at them—his inheritors, neither of whom would attain his majority, both of whom would die of the pox—in weeds at the edge of the empty house, in their clean clothing. **Q**

FAMILY
REPETITION

The Mine

Imagine me at twelve. The thin wrists, the bowed legs. I am sitting in the screened-in porch with my head cocked slightly to one side, as if to listen.

I am listening to the chimes.

I did not hear the story about my mother on purpose. It was an accident. It was an accident, too, when I rode that horse. I did not know that it was dying. It was sweating on the neck and sides. It staggered near the gate. Perhaps all horses do this, I thought. I remembered the stagger later, after the horse had died.

What I hear from the porch is what happened to my mother when she was thirty-one years old. She lived where I lived when I was twelve, in Bisbee, Arizona, in a town on the edge of a copper mine. The town itself is like a mine, the way the houses hang on steep ledges. The houses, the trees, even the churches hang from the sides like barnacles.

She was alone in the house. My father was in the mine, and my mother was alone in the house. I was in California with an aunt because my mother was ill. She became ill when she had me. That was in the summer, in July.

My mother walked down the thirty-two concrete steps that lead to the nearest road, but before she did that, she slit her wrists; she cut them on the back porch with my father's razor while he was in the mine—then she walked down the thirty-two concrete steps. All of them had been poured by hand.

I look a great deal like my mother. The thin wrists, the one eye that slants upward a little. You hardly notice the eye except in photographs. It becomes more apparent then. Just as the staggering became more apparent. I did not notice it until after the horse had died.

. . .

In Bisbee, the streets are too narrow for more than one car to pass. The streets climb steep hills; they wind, and on one side the steps climb still higher to the houses. Metal stakes have been driven into the walls to keep them from falling down. It would all fall down like cake if they had not driven these stakes into the walls.

I do not think our steps had a handrail all the way down. In places, you had to step without holding on to anything, and if it was winter, you could not go down that way. You had to walk through the trees to another road. It must have been fall when my mother walked down those steps. The steps were very steep, and in the fall, there were leaves on them.

I had stopped reading, and I was watching the chimes. I had remembered the time my mother said a snake slid down the chimes. She heard them move, she said, and when she looked out, she could see the snake on them.

My mother was not in the house the day I was sitting on the porch. Just an aunt and a friend of the family were there, a woman named Georgia Weeks. They must have been waiting for something.

I heard my aunt tell Georgia Weeks what happened.

I can't imagine, Georgia Weeks said, to go off and slit her wrists on the day the baby was to come home.

What did she have? my aunt said. Married that man at seventeen.

The horse was an accident. It died of an infection. I rode it only for an hour or so, until I noticed the sweating. I did not ride it much after that. She had been poked in the breast by a stick of some kind. It should have healed, it seemed to have healed, it seemed to be gone when I rode her.

I have never known another person whose mother was named Vanessa.

Every night at the Copper Queen Hotel I would go around and check the doors of the fire escapes. I was to check them every night after the restaurant closed. The pool below the back fire escape was shaped like a mouth, and from where I stood you could see Bisbee. You could see our house, steps. I used to wonder how someone could climb down the fire escape in the dark, with only the light of the pool to see by. The lights on the hill were no help. These were no help to me at all on the fire escape.

I counted the steps from our house on my way to the Copper Queen Hotel. In the winter, I went around the other way, but in the summer, I walked the thirty-two steps to the road. In places, the handrail stopped. My father had put a light for me at the top, as far as the cord would reach, just at the very top of the steps. My father always did that for me.

My aunt said he was a good man in many ways. She said that to Georgia Weeks. I heard the women talking through the screen door.

By the time I worked at the Copper Queen Hotel, my mother lived in Phoenix. My father lived in the same house he lived in when my mother walked down the steps. My father lived there until he died. I saw him take a drink once or twice, not much. He only drank when I poured it. That is the kind of man he was. The two of us would sit down to dinner on my day off, and I would pour us each a drink, and we would drink together, and I would play the piano afterward, because that is what my father liked. He liked "La Golondrina." I would play "La Golondrina," and my father would have one more drink. He never smoked in the house. That is one thing he never did.

Imagine my mother in Phoenix, a woman named Vanessa in a place like that. She lived on Oracle Street. There were palms in the courtyard, not a single hill, not a single step. It was a one-story affair.

Once, when I went to see her, she was ironing a piece of paper. When I got inside, I could see it was paper from a gift someone had given her. It was wrapping paper. And then there was the day she said let me get the bottles from the back, and she went to get the 7-Up bottles, and as she stood up, with a pack of them in each hand, she fell backward, straight back, like nothing I had ever seen, and her head hit the concrete.

The bottles fell into the pool.

She fell straight back.

The thin wrists, the bowed legs. You cannot tell now that my legs are bowed. It is very slight now. You can tell it in my mother, in the way that she stands. But the small slant of one eye is not apparent even in pictures taken of my mother now. You can see it only in the old pictures, in the one of her and me in Bisbee, before I left for California.

When my father got cancer, he closed his mouth. He never ate another bite. That is how he died.

Imagine my mother in Phoenix. The paper she ironed had hummingbirds on it, hummingbirds with small wings.

From the windows of the Copper Queen Hotel you could see the fence around the Presbyterian church. You could see the iron fence with its iron crosses. The iron crosses with the circles in the center. You could see this church from the patio, from the two or three tables outside. Bisbee is known for its climate. The signs that say this are outside the Lavender Pit copper mine. It is not big business now, just a gaping hole. You cannot imagine the size of it.

I could feel the horse breathing if I thought about it later. I could feel the horse taking deep breaths.

. . .

Imagine me at twelve. My mother saw the snake slip down. It never happened again while I was watching. I watched for it to happen, but it never did.

When I played "La Golondrina," he would sometimes sigh. I did not play it very often. Perhaps it was not every Sunday that we did that, when I played "La Golondrina" and he drank himself to sleep.

He loved to hear it.

I always planned to play it.

Every Sunday, I promised. **Q**

Swain Corliss, Hero of Malcolm's Mills
(Now Oakland, Ontario), November 6, 1814

In the morning, the men rubbed their eyes and saw Kentucky cavalry and Indians mounted on stolen farm horses cresting the hill on the opposite side of the valley. The Kentuckians looked weary and calm, their hollow eyes slitted with analysis. We were another problem to be solved; they had been solving problems all the way from Fort Detroit, mostly by killing, maiming, and burning, which were the usual methods.

The Indians were Cherokee and Kickapoo, with some Muncies thrown in. They had eagle-feather rosettes and long hair down the sides of their heads and paint on their faces, which looked feminine in that light. Some wore scalps hanging at their belts.

They came over the hill in a column, silent as the steam rising from their mounts, and stopped to chew plug tobacco or smoke clay pipes while they analyzed us. More Kentuckians coming on extended the line on either side of the track into the woods, dismounted, and started cook fires or fell asleep under their horses' bellies, with reins tied at the wrists.

General McArthur rode in with his staff, all dressed in blue, with brass buttons and dirty white facings. He spurred his mare to the front, where she shied and pranced and nearly fell on the steep downward incline. He gave a sign, and the Indians dismounted and walked down the road to push our pickets in. The Indians had an air of attending their eighty-seventh or so battle. They trudged down the dirt road bolt upright, with their muskets cradled, as though bored with the whole thing, as though they possessed some precise delineation of the zone of danger that bespoke a vast familiarity with death and dying.

The men who could count counted.

Somebody said, "Oh, sweet Baby Jesus, if there's a one, there must be a thousand."

I should say that we had about four hundred—the 1st and 2nd Norfolk Militia, some Oxfords and Lincolns, six instructors from the 41st Foot, and some local farmers who had come up the day before for the society.

Colonel Bostwick (the men called him Smiling Jack) stood higher up on the ridge behind our line, watching the enemy across the valley with a spyglass, his red coat flapping at his thighs. He stood alone mostly. He had been shot in the leg at Frenchman's Creek and in the face at Nanticoke when he walked into the Dunham place and stumbled on Sutherland and Onstone's gang by accident. The wound on his face made him look as though he were smiling all the time, which was repellent and unnerved his troops in a fight.

Injun George, an old Chippeway who kept house in a hut above Troyer's Flats, was first up from the creek. He said he had seen a black snake in the water, which was bad luck. He said the Kickapoo had disappeared when he shot at them, which meant that they had learned the disappearing trick and had strong medicine. He himself had been trying to disappear for years with little success. Later, he shot a crow off the mill roof, which he said was probably one of the Kickapoos.

A troop of Kentuckians came down the hill with ammunition pouches and Pennsylvania long rifles and started taking pot shots at McCall's company hiding behind a barricade of elm logs strung across the road. We could not reply much for lack of powder, so the Kentuckians stood out in the open on the stream bank, smoking their white clay pipes and firing up at us. Others merely watched, or pissed down the hill, or washed their shirts and hung them out to dry, as though fighting and killing were just another domestic chore, like slopping pigs or putting up preserves.

Somebody said, "They are just like us except that we are not in Kentucky lifting scalps and stealing horses and trying to take over the place."

The balls sounded like pure-D evil thunking into the logs.

Someone else tried to raise a yell for King George, which fell flat, many men allowing as it was a mystery why King George had drawn his regulars across to the other side of the Grand River and burned the ferry scow so that they could not be here when the fighting started.

Thunk, thunk went the balls. A melancholy rain began to fall, running in muddy rivulets down the dirt track. Smoke from the Republican cook fires drifted down into the valley and hung over the mill race.

Colonel Bostwick caused some consternation coming down to be with his men, marching up and down just behind the line with that strange double grin on his face (his cheek tattooed with powder burns embedded in the skin) and an old officer's spontoon across his shoulders, exhorting us in a hoarse, excited mutter.

"Behold, ye infidels, ye armies of Gog and Magog, agents and familiars of Azazel. Smite, smite! O Lord, bless the children who go into battle in thy name. Remember, boys, the Hebrew kings did not scruple to saw their enemies with saws and harrow them with harrows of iron."

Sergeant Major Collins of the 41st tried to make him lie down behind the snake fence, but the colonel shook him off, saying, "The men must see me." The sergeant took a spent ball in the forehead and went down. The ball bounced off, but he was dead nonetheless, a black knot sprouting between his brows like a third eye.

A sharpshooter with a good Pennsylvania Dutch long rifle can hit a man at three hundred yards, which is twice as far as any weapon we had could throw, let alone be accurate. So far we had killed only one crow, which might or might not have been an enemy Indian.

Edwin Barton said, "I dreamt of Tamson Mabee all night. I threw her down in the hay last August, but she kept her hand over her hair pie and wouldn't let me. She ain't hardly fourteen. I'll bet I'm going to hell today."

Somebody said, "You ever done it with a squaw? A squaw'll lay quiet and not go all herky-jerky like a white woman. I prefer a squaw to a white woman any day."

And somebody else said, "I know a man over at Port Rowan who prefers hogs for the same reason."

This was war and whiskey talking.

We lay in the rain dreaming of wives and lovers, seeking amnesty in the hot purity of lust—yes, some furtively masturbating in the rain with cold hands. Across the valley, the Kentuckians seemed like creatures of the autumn and of rain, their amphibian eyes slitty with analysis. Our officers, Salmon and Ryerson, said we held good ground, whatever that meant, that the American army at Niagara was already moving back across the river, that we had to stop McArthur from burning the mills of Norfolk so we could go on feeding King George's regulars.

Trapped in that valley, waiting for the demon cavalry to come whooping and shrieking across the swollen creek, we seemed to have entered some strange universe of curved space and strings of light. Rain fell in strings. Some of us were already dead, heroes of other wars and battles. We had been fighting now since August 8, 1812, when we went down the lake with Brock to the relief of Amherstburg. At times like these, we could foresee the mass extinction of the whole species, the world turned to a desert of glass.

Everything seemed familiar and inevitable. We had marched up from Culver's Tavern the day before. We had heard firing in the direction of Brant's Ford at dusk, and awakened to see Kentucky cavalry and Indians emerging from the forest road and smoke rising from barn fires back of them. Evidently, given their history, Kentuckians are born to arson and mayhem. Now they sniped with passionate precision (*thunk, thunk* went the balls), keeping us under cover while they moved troops down the steep bank.

Shielding our priming pans with our hats, we cursed the rain and passed the time calculating angles of assault. The mill pond, too deep except to swim, protected our left wing. That meant Salmon's boys would get hit first, thank goodness. Mrs. Malcolm and her Negro servant were busy moving trunks and armoires out of the house in case of fire—no one paid them any mind. All at once, we heard shouts and war cries deep in the woods downstream. Colonel Bostwick sent a scout, who returned a moment later to say McArthur's Indians had out-flanked us, crawling across a deadfall ford.

We stared at the clouds and saw fatherless youngsters weeping at the well, lonely widows sleeping with their hands tucked between their legs, and shadows moving with horrible wounds, arms or legs missing, brains dripping out their ears.

Someone said, "I can't stand this no more," stood up, and was shot in the spine, turning. He farted and lay on his face with his legs quivering. His legs shook like a snake with its back broken. The Kentuckians were throwing an amazing amount of hot lead our way.

The colonel smiled and shouted additional remarks against Azazel, then ordered McCall to stand at the elm-tree barricade while the rest retired. This was good news for us. We could get by without the mills of Norfolk; it was our bodies, our limbs, lungs, nerves, and intestines we depended on for today and tomorrow.

McCall had Jo Kitchen, a noted pugilist, three of the Austin brothers, Edwin Barton, and some others. We left them our powder and shot, which was ample for a few men. At the top of the valley, Swain Corliss turned back, cursing some of us who had begun to run. "Save your horses first, boys, and, if you can, your women!" He was drunk. Many of us did not stop till we reached home, which is why they sometimes call this the Battle of the Foot Race.

Swain Corliss hailed from a family of violent Baptists with farms on the Boston Creek about three miles from Malcolm's. His brother Ashur had been wounded thirteen times in the war and had stood his ground at Lundy's Lane, which Swain had missed on account of ague. Swain did not much like his brother getting ahead of him like that.

He had a Brown Bess musket and a long-barreled dragoon pistol his father had bought broken from an officer. He turned at the top of the hill and started down into the racket of lead and Indian shouts. Musket balls swarmed round McCall's company like bees, some stinging. Swain took up a position against a tree, guarding the flank, and started flinging lead back. Edwin Barton, shot through the thighs, loaded for him. Men kept getting up to leave and Captain McCall would whack them over the shoulders with the flat of his sword.

Swain Corliss, pounding a rock into the barrel of his gun with a wooden mallet, kept saying, "Boys, she may be rough, but she sure is regular."

Bees stung him.

That night, his father dreaming, dreamed a bee stung him in the throat and knew. Swain Corliss was catching up to Ashur. He killed a Kentucky private coming over the creek on a cart horse. Then Swain Corliss shot the horse. Smoke emerged from the mill. Mrs. Malcolm ran around in a circle, fanning the smoke with a linen cloth. (*Thunk, thunk, buzz, buzz* went the balls.) Though we were running, we were with them. It was our boys fighting in the hollow. Colonel Bostwick sat on his race horse, Governor, at the top of the track.

The company gave ground, turning to fire every few yards. Martin Boughner tied a handkerchief to his ramrod and surrendered to an Indian. Swain Corliss tied up Edwin Barton's legs with his homespun shirt. Deaf from the guns, they had to shout.

"By the Jesus, Ned, I do believe it ain't hard to kill them when they stand around you like this."

"I mind a whore I knew in Chippawa—"

"Ned, I wished you'd stop bleeding so freely. I think they have kilt you."

"Yes."

They were in another place, a region of black light and maximum density. On the road, sweating with shame in the cold, we heard the muskets dwindle and go out. We saw Swain

Corliss, white-faced, slumped against an oak amongst the dead smoldering leaves, Edwin's head in his lap, without a weapon except for his bayonet, which he held across his chest as Kickapoo warriors came up one by one, reverently touching Swain's shoulders with their musket barrels.

The Kentuckians had lost one dead, eight wounded, and a couple of borrowed horses. That day, they burned the mill and one downstream and sent out patrols to catch stragglers, which they did, and then released after making them promise on the Good Book not to shoot at another person from the United States. The Indians skinned and butchered Edwin Barton's body, Ned having no further use for it.

During the night, three miles away, James Corliss dreamed that a venomous bee had stung him in the throat. Rising from his bed, he told the family, "Yonder, yer baby boy is dead or something." Then James Corliss went out into the darkness, hitched his horse to a sled, placed a feather tick, pillows, and sheets upon it, and started for the scene of the battle. Q

Love, Love

I think Bruno sees things in the TV set. Don't ask me what. He walks up to the screen and tilts his head from side to side. I mean, it's a blank picture, no sound, the TV's off. Still, I think Bruno's picking up something. Bruno sits for a while, nose to the set, smudges the screen, sighs, lies down on the floor, and whimpers.

My psychiatrist says that Bruno is experiencing my depression. "Maybe he's looking for your husband," she says. "What do you think?"

I think for a while, look out her window, begin to cry. Dr. Vortz hands me a pink, rose-scented Kleenex, settles back in her chair, looks me straight in the eye. One hour every week we do this, while Bruno waits in the car. I bring him with me for the ride to her office. Bruno sits with his rump on the floor and his front paws on the seat and his head in my lap.

I don't lie down on Dr. Vortz's couch. Sometimes I'd like to. It looks inviting. It occurs to me it would feel nice to relax on the soft leather. But I can't. So I sit here, across from Dr. Vortz. Our feet might even touch, only hers are up on a footstool; thick ankles, heavy legs, Oriental rug on the floor between us. I gaze at the colors, let them flow and blur, let them swirl in the silence I sometimes make when I lose the rhythm of talking, run out of things to say. I stare at the rug and look up to catch Dr. V.'s eyes slipping, her head nodding a notch.

She's asleep. I should be angry.

But I feel ashamed.

"Are these sessions *doing* anything?" my mother wants to know. "Do you think they're *helping*?"

Every night after a session, my mother calls. She calls to see if the sessions are taking. I try to explain to my mother that improvement comes with time. I tell her, "It's a matter of working out the conflicts."

My mother is skeptical. She thinks I'm paying too much money—and she may be right. I am forty-one and she still gives me food when I leave her house to drive ten blocks away to mine. "For *later,*" she says. "For *Bruno.*"

The dog eats everything. He is relentless, not at all fussy. He won't beg, but he's ever watchful for a handout. And he'll perform at the drop of a hat. Bruno can balance anything on his nose—a pretzel, a kibble, a piece of meat, a grape—poised in quivering anticipation until you say it's okay for him to fling the food airborne and catch it.

Bruno was Harold's dog. Bruno came with the marriage, along with Harold's live paraphernalia—Harold's rabbits, mice, doves, peacock. I gave them all away except for Bruno. I couldn't stand to see them.

"So, the *psychiatrist,* is she helping?" Mother wants to know.

In the background I hear the theme song and the sound of applause as someone guesses right.

"Are you watching the *Wheel?*" she says.

"Go ahead," I tell her. "I'll talk to you later."

"Love, love," my mother says.

I once told Harold he should go on *Wheel of Fortune* and win us an incredible amount of money because that would impress my parents, that would show them. Because my parents, you see, never believed in Harold; they never saw in him what I saw. I wanted them to admire Harold. I wanted them to know how good Harold was, how uncommon. As it was, however, they thought of him as a clown. "How's No-No the Clown?" they'd say. They'd say it to his face and everyone would laugh. They said that it was all in fun, but I did not think it was funny. Harold wasn't stupid. Harold wasn't a joke. He just wanted to perform. Sure, his tricks were hokey, I admit it. He wore a black turtleneck sweater and black slacks and white cotton gloves. He did the standards—milk appearing and disappearing in a jug, a bouquet of flowers from a roll of newspaper, the vanishing quarter, the blank coloring book that with a wave of his wand was fully colored in. Okay, he wasn't very good. He was a mediocre magician, good enough for children's birthday parties, quick enough to fool them.

Billed as Mr. Presto.

Sometimes I'd go along on his jobs. I'd stand in the back with the mothers and watch Harold perform. I tried to be objective. I tried to forget that Harold was anyone special to me. I observed him, his effect on the children—the way he could hold them quiet, wide-mouthed, sitting up on their knees to see. And I watched the mothers, too—Harold's effect on them. I listened for bits of their conversations—innuendos about the size of Mr. Presto's wand.

I don't know how Harold stood those awful parties, why he sought them out. His job—he was a licensed electrician—was a perfectly good job; the income was ample for the two of us. I just don't know how Harold endured those children—always whining, always wanting more of something they weren't supposed to have.

But it's funny about Harold. That time when Macey Platts was missing and he knew just where to look. She was a little girl who lived down the street. She was five years old. "They'll find her in a trash dump over on Edmunds," he told me. He knew it, Harold knew it just like smelling the wind, just like knowing it's going to rain. It had come to him, I guess.

I made him call the police. "Just be anonymous," I said.

When it turned out that Harold was right, I started reading about psychics, people who claim to have some special faculty, some receiver-frequency relationship with things like yogurt and plants.

I'd say to Harold for him to show me how it's done, teach me the secrets. But he never would. It was something he'd share only with Bruno, the two of them alone in the den, practicing at all hours of the night. I'd hear the snap of the scarves, the baton unspring its coil, the cooing of the doves, and Bruno, tail thumping, so quick to please, so desirous of giving attention.

I waited six hours after Harold didn't come home. Then I called the police. They told me not to worry. But I worried. They said, "Don't worry." They said, "Nine out of ten husbands eventually show up."

After Harold disappeared, I tried to get in touch, I tried to find him. I thought, Maybe he's hurt and can't get home and needs me to help him. I read more books about these things, how to find your long-lost love. But I still have not found Harold. I have not found anything remotely related to Harold. The only thing I found was a red lion, in a dream I had; his mouth was open, his teeth dripping with blood.

But hey, look, Harold, if you want someone else, just come and tell me. Harold, if you're in trouble, Bruno and I are looking and listening for you.

Please materialize, Harold—we need to know! **Q**

Seven Years of Bad Words

She stayed in the room at the top of the house. She was writing *The Book of Rage*.

Her daughters called, Flea Flea! Flea-ma!

She pounded her piano leg on the ceiling.

Every day was like every day.

At night, the new timber wolves came close to the house, and anyone in the house could hear the juice running in their throats like the river running at the rapids toward the end of a dry season.

When it stormed, their hair stood on end. The lights went out and they took showers so they could feel the electricity going through their bodies and feel how exciting it would be to die. To hear the silver in our teeth sing.

They drove around in the big hot Cadillac with Delicious Grace and Gogo Live Forever, whose hands had already turned pink and who now had dizzy spells, who could no longer hear them, whose eardrums were tattered, whose hearing aid had given up the ghost, whose corroded emergency battery lay beside the penny and the one crumbling aspirin in the aspirin tin he stored in his side shirt pocket in order to be prepared for anything, who said sometimes at dinner where he was starving to death because his throat no longer swallowed that in seven years he would be two hundred years old, that he would die before them, that they would outlive him, that he would even die, raising his glass now, hear hear, before Delicious Grace! Who said, Oh, for God's sake, I could be struck by lightning tomorrow.

They drove around on the dirt roads and through the narrow fire lanes and over the flat blacktop highways and looked through the slowly chilling summer windows at the wildflowers growing in the ditches and the shadows of the crows' wings coming in from the back swamps and said, Maybe we should go to the South of France, but nobody paid any attention to that because they were not going to the South of France but right here to Cable to buy gas and to Butternut to buy chickens and to Ashland to be shot at by the Indians.

In the mornings, they could see their breath and the grass was stiff and the lake took the hair off the tops of their heads.

What's piano legs, Flea's daughters wanted to know.

The Flea had a piano leg and Ubangi hair, which Delicious Grace said was her problem and why she had no success with men. Delicious Grace said the leg was like this. Straight down. No ankle. No hope. Haven't you ever seen a piano? And what's a Ubangi? Delicious Grace said she had no idea. That's an expression. But you have to look right. You can't have hair like that. You can't go around like that. You can't just let it stick out. You won't get into a sorority that way. You don't go to tea dances that way. You have a sad life.

Flea-ma sat up there in the red dress she called her tent, her caftan, her last mobile home, and waited. She leaned forward over the table. She closed her eyes and breathed with her ribs. She never wrote anything down on paper. She sat at the table preparing. Once, after seven years, she said, I think there will be a word sometime soon. But I don't know. She said it depended on the weather. It depended on the Colonel. It depended on her hands. The palms of her hands were hot. If they cooled off, she would be able. Her hands looked like a baby's hands on one side and five-hundred-year-old blue on the other side. She said it depended on magic. It depended.

How would the words look, they wondered.

Like this. If you made a hole in your head with a wire, it would pierce the nest of words in there and they would come out onto the table. They would come out like baby spiders from a nest on your face. A swollen place and then a warm air on it and birth and spiders spilling out onto the table. The words would come out like that. Frail. Scattered. Skidding. And they would be so attracted to each other, so repelled by each other, so lively, so fiery. Such dancers. Or the words would come like ants marching, through an opening that appeared to be a trapdoor. The staircase would descend and upon it the ants, progressing with such fierce determination, with mad inexorability, with an appetite no longer containable, down down one after another, row after row lining up at attention, shoulder to shoulder, until a halt was called or until a retreat was ordered and the march back up the stairway was accomplished and the stairway was raised and the trapdoor closed and the latch secured.

It was her daughters who arranged to track the Colonel down and bring him to Flea, and when they did, she looked through the binoculars to where he was stretched out at the end of the mile-long pier and thought he must be dead. He had an apple in his mouth and flowers on his chest and his whole body was painted red and blue and there were lovely bits of beach glass and Coca-Cola bottle glass softened and rounded at the edges and interesting bottle tops from local beers with scrawled names of Linekskugel and Ojibwa on them all carefully pasted onto the Colonel's heavenly appendages so that he glittered and sparkled in the noon sun, and he had flippers on his feet and a spear in his hand and in his arms a hook for fish and a respirator and a mouthpiece and a tank for compressed air that had never been filled.

The sight of the Colonel made the Flea think about the story the man at the pool at the Holiday Inn outside of Chicago had told years before of the summer of the runaway tank when the diver had failed to check his tank and it had taken off and exploded and gone right through the trunk of the car and through the car itself and up through the windshield and through the garage out there at the little house and into the kitchen and down into the family room and to its resting place right there beside the trunk of the plastic palm. Always check your tank, the bald instructor told them.

Gazing down on the Colonel, she thought he must be dead because he was so big and still and because the boat was decorated to look like the funeral barges she and her daughters had seen during their travels and like the raft they had built for themselves one winter on the Gulf. The daughters had brought the sleeping or dead Colonel across the lake on the bateau on pontoons and decorated it so that it no longer looked like a floating crap game with captain's chairs around the card table and poor white trash hanging off the sides screaming. We can cut down all the trees we want, we can paint the birches silver, we can make them Day-Glo, we can shave the grass if we want to, our daddy knows the Bears, our daddy owns a bar, our daddy owns the Turk's down by Grandview. Now the bateau had a white awning and striped cushions and a fleet of red canoes with campers dressed like Indians following it and a three-piece band playing "In the Land of the Sky Blue Waters" and the cousins in their own small feather boat with the battery-operated motor whirring and going around and around and around and making the goggle-eyed cousins look happy but dizzy and the sweet little seaplane circling, dipping a wing, sending out smoke rings, unfurling a string of smoky words they had not seen in seven years.

All that time, the Flea had been up there in the room at the top of the house writing *The Book of Rage* and thinking about the Colonel, calling, Hey, Colonel, hey, Warrior. Where is you? Hey, you all, come on down back up here now. I is calling you. I is de mudduh. I is de river rat. There was something about the Colonel that made her change her way of speaking. Why you talk that way, her daughters said. You sound like a car wreck. You sound like a southbound train. Colonel Savior, she called. Colonel Airman Parachute Man, long slender beautiful legs Colonel. Colonel Swollen Lips. Colonel Delicious. Colonel fighting man, bomb dropping, doctoring, healing, sunburned-neck Colonel. Come back. Colonel legs as thin as mints, Colonel you all.

On several occasions, Flea's daughters found pictures of the Colonel in the Sunday magazine sections, and once they found a story about him in a Guatemalan paper and another time in the *Thailand Gazette,* which they subscribed to when they began working to track him down and on whose faded pages he was shown carrying children he had discovered floating in the South China Sea, looking pale, Flea thought, looking like flan. Once they received a letter from Air Force headquarters in Colorado informing them that the colonel they were seeking sounded very much like a colonel in California. That address was confidential, but they were encouraged to proceed with the correspondence and were promised that the letters would be forwarded.

They proceeded. Dear Colonel. Dear sweet bloody tongue Colonel, we are ready to go with you, our mother is ready, big Mumbles, the woman who is no bigger than a flea, our Flea is ready, our Flea-ma, please respond, we include photographs of you in the little cardboard city you built with our Flea-ma in the desert outside of La Paz when the dam broke and the children washed out to sea and the harbor was in quarantine and the tropical-fish salesmen and the missionary and the real nurse and you who had dropped out of the sky in a blue-and-red plane formed a salvation team and began to build paper houses and put showers on the trees and eye drops in the eyes and salve on the lips and fish the bloated dogs out of the bay and the fruit-picking poor dead workers out of the bay and our Flea-ma came into town and saw the soldiers sweeping with brooms made of straw and the windows boarded up and the malacon split in half with the sea shooting up through the cracks and the yachts of the sportsmen going down and stopped in the only hotel in the town that was open and went into the courtyard where the hat floated on the surface of the swimming pool and the tables rattled in the wind and the great gray fountain dripped like a great gray leaky wedding cake and met you coming across the courtyard and heard you say, You must be the new nurse.

The New Nurse. On breezy nights, when Delicious Grace made Minnesota Mudballs with five-star Barbancourt rum and Courvoisier, they would take the handmade pottery tumblers from Clam Lake up to Flea-ma's room and she would lean back in her tractor chair and elaborate. Small she was, with the piano leg and the Ubangi hair, but as fierce as any war hero, and bigger than General William Walker, their Tennessee journalist revolutionary namesake, who had taken over that same port city where she had so rapidly fallen into the Colonel's arms more than one hundred years ago, only to fail in his brief reign as dictator and die a disgraceful and violent death by firing squad in Honduras. A traveler in her great-great-cousin's lost city, the Flea had stood in her white cotton pants and white shirt and espadrilles, oddly, magically, dressed already in the uniform of her next profession when before her always expectant, occasionally hopeful, sometimes bloodshot eyes had sprung the Colonel, also with bloodshot eyes, but so delicious, smelling of war and calamine lotion, which she the Flea still smelled on certain Indian-summer afternoons, and looking at her with a feverish intensity that showed the first fires of the universe still burning, whose even white teeth already biting down on her red Wisconsin lips had caused Flea to give up like that, with a little shiver and a rumble in her throat any would-be Explorer's Cruise for the purpose of studying plant life and salt panning and black jackrabbits and celestial navigation and the habits of the shark fishermen who roamed the red sea waters of the Gulf. After the Colonel, the Flea's ticket for the sailing expedition rotted with the salt tablets and the lucite evening slippers with the goldfish cavorting in the heels. The pencil with which she had planned to make scientific notations was eaten by a Mexican mouse and the straw hat she had bought to wear on the deck of the cruise ship was lost in a high wind and thrown into a dustbin by the real nurse, who continued to provide real Scotch for the Colonel and real though fiercely muscular and wildly hairy arms, which appeared to frighten him, and who without much delay managed to develop a lifelong desire for revenge against the Flea. That scheming half-pint, that wooden gnat, the real nurse sometimes hissed. That Midwestern stringray, that slug.

Tell about the days, the daughters would say. From the beginning. From the dawn! I don't think people are interested in that part, Delicious Grace would say. You may be, but I can assure you that other people don't want to know.

The Flea would roll her eyes. Nevertheless. She would lick her lips. Nevertheless. She would pound the piano leg on the floor until Gogo Live Forever took a canoe paddle down there where he was reading and underlining the important parts in *The History of the World as Seen from the Middle West* and send it up through a crack in the ceiling.

The days began at dawn, when they opened the shutters and stood on their balcony wrapped in torn sheets and shreds of Mexican tapestry and now and then a stray curtain and went right on to building houses and bandaging and distributing medicines and photographing, the role of photojournalist having been undertaken by the Flea, who went nowhere on earth without her Canon F-1 and who was therefore responsible for the photographs published throughout the world of the Colonel waving and making a V sign and the tropical-fish salesmen building their cardboard city and the missionary throwing stones at the Red Cross truck because the Colonel refused to let him head the rescue team even though he had driven the truck on the motorcycle trail down the entire length of Baja and was eighty-two and had no teeth, and the photographs of the Colonel and Flea on self-timer drinking Dos Equis beer and rubbing bare toes beneath the table at the restaurant where the American woman and her retired matador husband served cheeseburgers for which the woman was homesick, and the photograph of the Colonel and the Mayor shaking hands in front of the new resort hotel in which the windows had been blown out and where the remnants of yellow silk billowed out toward the sea every evening when the *coromuel* breeze came up in the west, and finally the underexposed photograph of the balcony overlooking the courtyard of the hotel where Flea-ma and the Colonel had been the only guests, where late at night they had listened to the dogs barking and shutters slamming and the radio playing on the Hertz woman's desk where the sign in gold letters on mahogany said INQUIRE WITHIN ABOUT TRIPS TO THE INTERIOR.

Three cheers for Flea-ma, the daughters would say on those nights. Hooray for our Flea. And Delicious Grace would pour more mudballs and remind her daughter that nothing good had ever come of that kind of activity and nothing ever would, and far below them in his reading room Gogo Live Forever, who went on telling himself the tale of the History of the World with lips that moved but made no sound, would listen for news, for a wind stirring in the birches, for the distant thunder of a summer storm, for the rain coming, for the quickness of death.

If the bateau carrying the Colonel on that summer afternoon in the land of the sky-blue waters where Flea hovered over *The Book of Rage* had been allowed to land at the pier, if the Flea had come from her room at the top of the house to embrace her love in time, if Gogo Live Forever had not made his way down from the big house to the boathouse and out along the mile-long pier to say that this was not permitted, this kind of landing, this kind of boat, this flaming entourage, this flower pot, this flowered funeral parlor, they weren't having anything to do with finales here, change the subject, get onto something more cheerful, talk about something we can all enjoy, get off that, stop rubbing it in, stop waving it before him; if the seaplane had not come in too close for a landing and if the string of words fluttering behind it had not caught in the bateau's motor and triggered a series of collisions and explosions and a fire that moved on paths of gasoline down the mile-long pier to the boathouse and along the shoreline through the birches and pines to the house, the ending would have been the same.

As it was, the Colonel woke to find himself in a serious situation and took the apple out of his mouth immediately. All of his life he had been preparing for crises and he was not a Colonel and a former war hero and now a worldwide savior of helpless and weary people and a worldwide lover of sometimes beautiful and always enthusiastic women for nothing, and he was not going to end his days with bottle tops glued to his chest and flippers on his feet in the land of the sky-blue waters with the man who would live forever shouting at him and shaking a split canoe paddle. Fuck it. If there was one thing he hated, it was a place north of the Tropic of Cancer, and he was far above it now and there were flowers around his legs and a tank in his arms. He went overboard. He went under.

Gogo Live Forever and Delicious Grace and Flea's daughters and the pilot of the seaplane and two of the small cousins and the pilot of the bateau hired at the Ojibwa reservation who was in every way except for black eyes and a meaner set to her jaw the exact replica of the real nurse in La Paz went after him and were not seen again either, though occasionally the Flea received hints of their whereabouts.

Local gossip held that ghosts of the whole preposterous bunch were repeatedly seen in the ice blocks that were cut each winter and carried up to the ice houses and covered with sawdust until the summer when the blocks were hosed off and chipped into the brilliant clear shards that went into ice buckets and ice-cream makers and into the mouths of children. But the Flea continued to receive what she believed to be talismans from Southeast Asia, tiny packages from Spain, once a wristwatch with Chinese numbers, once a postcard from Tierra del Fuego, and once on a birchbark canoe sent from no farther away than Butternut the words of warning or perhaps prophecy that had streamed behind the seaplane on the day of the conflagration. You can tell tales till your tongue melts. You can tell them forever.

During an early spring, a poster with a photograph of the real nurse without hair now or eyebrows announced a slide program on the need for purer water, and when the ice was cut one winter, a block delivered to the Corner Bar offered one perfectly preserved signet ring with the Colonel's initials, followed not long afterward by a request for the ring from a man in the costume of priest or Indian brave. He wore a blanket or cape or cloak, the bartender reported. He spoke another language. He rotated clockwise on the balls of his feet.

The Flea wrote slowly. In her own language. In a plywood tepee with a bed and a table and a toaster oven. Wearing the cap of her lost family that fit close to her head and held a hundred holes for the feathers they had once worn with such pleasure and pride, saying to one another as they put them in, Another feather in my cap, good, yes, very good. She worked slowly, persistently, without hope or doubt. The words proceeded and she acknowledged once in a note to the architect overseeing the rebuilding of the old house that the trick was to go on, day by day. To get up. To sit down, to begin, to begin again, to proceed. To be lonely, failed, deaf, lame, a drinker, a dreamer, a squanderer. And still to proceed. And to watch with a combination of horror and something approaching joy the procession of words, the long march, the madness of the dance, and as she went on, the occasional hint of the rage giving way, of something in her easing, something healing, something breaking up, unfolding and changing and continuing as the land did, as the seasons did, as one season withdrew and another unfolded, as one pulled in and another gave unto, as winter drifted slowly into spring and spring into summer and fall and winter and spring again, over and over, forever and ever, even as they came one by one to the shore of the lake and bowed down to plant the last shadows of the seeds of their beginnings on the surface of the frozen waters. **Q**

Summer Romance

I went to the airport to meet my cousin, a French girl. I drove like a lunatic, spinning through Van Wyck traffic.

I'd met Anne six summers before, when she was twelve, a doll. I'm twenty-three. She was just—you know what we mean—just a friend. There had never been anything more between us. The rest of it we talked ourselves into.

Over the years, I wrote her plenty of letters and asked her for pictures. She sent lots, and at first they were posed and graceless, but she was still beautiful. Later, she went through a coy period, when the pictures stopped coming altogether, and then a flamboyant time, when she was almost naked.

She was getting into it, I think, though she may have been a little unstable. Anyway, I cut out my favorite parts and made a giant collage of them.

I had spent the last four months of my life campaigning for her to come over for the summer. My mom was lending me the car and I had saved enough money for a long trip. Her parents finally said okay.

Then I had to convince Anne of the idea.

Please come, I wrote. I love you. I love you. I wonder could you send me a nude picture, you know, or one with just your tits naked at least. Please come.

It isn't a matter of getting what you want or not. Most people are used to living with what they don't get. It's a matter of what you tell yourself and of what you pretend. That's what I learned.

The plane was late. Then three charter flights landed at the same gate at once, including hers. But no Anne. I went through a couple of doors and hallways I wasn't supposed to and stopped in front of two cops wearing sunglasses.

"I'm waiting for my cousin," I explained, knowing it sounded like a lie and not being able to prove anything, either. "Do you think she might be in there?" I said.

"See the game last night?" asked the cop.

"Fell asleep," the other cop said.

A woman at the Air France counter took pity on my wretched face and went to check for me. "There's no girl that looks like that in there," she said.

Maybe she's a blonde now, or she got a little taller, or maybe she changed her name. I was almost crying.

Only my fundamental belief in my own worthiness prevented me from deliberately crashing my car against a Van Wyck Expressway guardrail

There was no answer at her apartment, or at her grandparents', just unfathomable, depthless, intercontinental clickings on the telephone line.

I slept fitfully next to the phone. It rang constantly, except when I awoke.

"Didn't she tell you?"—shocked French voice in struggling English. "She cannot come. We found the results of some exams. She lied to us, you understand, so we couldn't let her leave. We can't reward lying, you understand."

Sure, I understood. I was of course a mature adult.

Poor child.

A week later, when she arrived at Kennedy, and she seemed—at least she could walk—okay, I could hardly notice the effects of her feeble suicide attempt.

"You must be warm," my mom said to her.

"I'm fine," Anne said. Her long-sleeved sweater hid her wrists. She was sweating like a drug addict with the bends.

She called her parents to tell them she was in New York.

"I won't say it," she said. "No. I'm not sorry," she said. "I'm not."

She hung up. She laughed. "They've cut off my allowance," she said.

I stood there with my hands slightly outstretched, like a seller at the flea market who has just placed a porcelain rocking chair on a narrow glass shelf.

For me! I thought, though I was embarrassed to think like that. For me! She almost killed herself for my sake!

There it was, though, the truth, and what girl wouldn't?

We were supposed to stop in Cairo, Kentucky, to visit my relative Paul. We picked up a hitchhiker in New Jersey.

"Come with me to Frisco instead," the hitchhiker said. "You can stay with me and my friends."

"We have to go," I said. "We're expected." And besides, the whole idea sounded dangerous to me. I figured I'd tell the hitcher to get lost.

"*You* don't have to go," she said, pulling at Anne's hair.

"Okay," Anne said, "I want to go to Frisco."

I sneezed. Be reasonable, I thought.

"Okay, but let's stop in Cairo along the way," I said.

"I don't want to stop in Cairo," Anne said.

Women get their orders from outer space.

"You can stop if you want. We'll go ourselves and you can meet us," the hitcher said.

Right. Hi, Paul. Anne is on her way to San Francisco with a lesbian hitchhiker we met on the Jersey Turnpike.

"Nah," I said, throwing caution to the wind.

We were sick of sleeping in the car, so I got us a motel room somewhere in Utah. The highway was breathtaking and all that crap.

I called Paul from a phone booth.

"We're in Utah," I said. "We missed Kentucky."

"You missed it? Do you honestly expect me to believe that you just missed it?"

"Sort of. We'll stop on our way," I said.

When I got back to the room, Anne and the hitcher still had their clothes on, but they were lying on the bed, kissing and roaming.

I back-pedaled out the door and went to the bar.

A guy made conversation for an hour, and I didn't understand a word. Then he went away.

A woman came in and announced, "What I wouldn't do for a real man."

There was no one else. I felt bold.

She said, "You're not a virgin, are you? I'm a lover, not a teacher. Last one I had, he blew chunks all over himself, if you'll excuse my French."

There was a DO NOT DISTURB sign on our door.

"I'm going for a walk," I announced through the door.

"Okay!" I heard the hitcher call back.

"Don't worry if I'm late," I said.

"Okay!" I heard the hitcher say.

"Maybe I'll sleep in the car," I said.

"Whatever," I heard the hitcher say.

The lady's house somewhere in Utah.

"Straight or on ice?"

"I thought that was my job." I laughed easily, like no virgin, taking the bottle from her hands. Our fingers grazed sexually.

Later.

"Pour me another," the woman hiccupped—brazenly, I guess.

"Maybe you shouldn't," I said, letting the flea-market antique dealer in me get the upper hand.

"Give me the fucking bottle."

I sneezed.

We slept side by side that night. That kind of thing happens to me a lot. I've gotten used to it. She scratched my foot with her toenail in her sleep. I woke up early.

"It's great waking up next to someone in the morning," she said.

Yeah.

I knocked on the door.

"G'way," I heard someone say.

The only thing open was the truckstop, and not the romantic brunch food Eastern yuppies dream of. It was inedible. I tried refusing to pay, but I was threatened, so I paid.

I was still hungry.

The motel restaurant opened. Anne and the hitcher came down, showered, pert.

The hitcher insisted on paying the motel bill.

In Nevada, she said, "You should have joined us."

"I didn't know," I said.

She sighed wearily.

I cursed myself up and down for being so dumb. But how was I supposed to know?

"How about tonight?" I asked.

"Ernie," the hitcher said dryly, with patience patience patience, "try to stop planning things five years at a time. Leave that to the Chinese."

Anne laughed. Of course.

"We may all be dead by tonight," the hitcher added.

After that, I drove with extreme caution.

I couldn't tell you where the house was. We stayed only three days. I never drove out for groceries and the people in the house talked about The Haight like it was in the next county, so all I'm sure about is we weren't there.

It was three stories, two bathrooms, a monster living room, and skayty-eight bedrooms.

They talked as if the sixties were still going on.

No.

They talked as if everything had just ended. As if there were fresh scores to be settled. As if it still mattered who was right. As if apathy was still the major obstacle we were all talking about.

Nostalgic for when they were just starting to be nostalgic.

Rubbing the sands of time in old wounds.

Hey, you people had your chance. You blew it. Fuck you. Move over. You had the right idea. But let me at it.

I was draped in the mantle of my own brilliant self-pity. Everyone else was sitting around smoking something. Anne sat on the couch with her hand in the hitcher's lap. This was all just a romantically typical American scene Anne had probably been dreaming about. Her parents had been right, I thought.

She sprang off the couch and stretched like a young animal.

They were passing around an old argument.

I left.

I'm better off when I'm alone, almost at ease with myself. I was alone in my room. Masturbating, but so what?

A girl simultaneously knocked and entered.

"Hi," I said, stopping, but making no other effort.

"Whatcha up to?" she asked, sitting on my bed.

"Nothing. You know. Jerking off."

We sort of laughed.

"I think you're cute," she said. "Kind of square, but cute."

"I feel square," I said.

"Maybe, like, we could make it sometime. You know, get it on."

"Why wait?" I wondered.

"Now isn't the time," she said. "I think your friend is kind of in trouble."

"Cousin," I said.

Anne was on the couch, the hitcher on one side and the house guru on the other. They seemed intense, helping, and calm. Anne especially seemed calm. Asleep, in fact.

They pushed a Styrofoam cup of coffee at her lips, tilted her head, forced open her lips, and poured.

She gagged.

They slapped her a little. Kind of too hard, I thought.

"Someone should call a doctor," I said.

"It's been done," the guru said firmly, like shut up.

Shut up. Shut the fuck up. Shut the fuck up. Shut up.

Her eyes opened and sort of rolled around in the sockets. She spoke softly, pausing lifetimes. "I know. I know. It's okay. I'll be okay."

Then her eyes shut and we knew she would not be okay.

I could picture trying to explain on the phone to Paris. I thought they were vitamins.

They were all very calm, except for the precision and violence of their slaps and the attempts to make her heart beat again.

Hit her again! I thought, watching.

Aside from the phone calls, it was easy to get over her. I mean, what can feel worse than that Sunday night when you know there's no way in the world you're handing your homework in on time? That's the truly awful thing. No one has the decency to tell you when you're ten, "Kid, it'll never feel any worse than this."

So I'm telling. **Q**

An Imperishable Romance

I've been trying to get hold of someone to have some fun with. They both have. Let's pretend nothing is awkward. Three of us abreast, with the ancient and august chapel behind us, and in front of us the alarm was not so great. It was the moon. When he squealed about the moon, what I said was "You should have seen it this afternoon! It was so big and red!"

I had made a mistake.

The crux of her advice about walking in the cold toward our car, way down the road, was "You just have to do it." We were not dressed for the cold. As a group, we had looked at her black suede French oxfords because we had wanted to, and she didn't want to get them ruined in the dark. She watched her step. I watched my boots. Yes, they sank into the grass at least an inch, not out of sight. I had told him which of his shoes to be wearing. When we were alone, I had spoken to him while tapping, "I like this and this and this."

Certain things should not be spoken of in front of children. I agree with that. Children should not do certain things, and I agree with that. Thank God, she ran like hell, once out of the car, at her house.

It's a Japanese lantern hanging up there—wildly picturesque—before you get to her front door. Has this person never heard of a *bood*?—my favorite word for it. Q

Peniel

The child who became a very great president of the United States of America scolded Dr. Tiffany: "You got me in the eye!" because some of the novocaine Tiffany withdrew with his syringe needle from a vial shot into the child's eye on account of the doctor's clumsiness, and the doctor knew it.

For these purposes, *a very great president* means a president who understands the meaning of the word *good* and who is capable of leading the country, and therefore the world, at least several giant steps toward *Good*.

After the child was shot, Dr. Tiffany commanded the child, "Don't move, that's all you have to do."

The nurse attending both of them, holding the vial, was acting as a nurse for one day only. On all other days the nurse was a fireman at the army base.

There had been another nurse attending also, but she had been jubilant to excuse herself: "You know what to get him!" she volleyed at the fireman; then she had taken off, as if she was flying.

When she did so jubilantly, the child was doing a quick, wild writhe after having been shot. He was lying down. Dr. Tiffany was standing big and tall—the tallest one, with a robin's-egg-blue paper mask, masking half his face, tied behind his head, and the abashed fireman was confronting Dr. Tiffany.

So far the clues are: the word *Tiffany* probably from *theophany; robin's-egg-blue; fireman;* and *vial*—the same sound as *vile*.

Whoops, before the presentation of clues, more information should have appeared concerning the child—that the child repeated—he scolded the doctor again.

Dr. Tiffany reiterated, "Trust me, trust me. It's safe, I

know, in your eye—because we put it in eyedrops. That's how
.I know.''

The fireman was too abashed to speak.

The fireman never in his life told anyone either the partic-
ulars of his masturbatory techniques, and they were manifestly
soothing inventions. The fireman knew how to feel as if he was
with someone he could love when he was all alone. He should
have told at least one other person how. **Q**

She would
Never be
called a
small
Town
Girl
again

The Word

And God said, Son,
you won't be a teenager
forever. You'll live
33 years, die hard.
In between you'll work
some miracles, spread
The Word.
And Jesus said, Dad,
can't I just get one lousy
blowjob?

Sun Kills; Acid Rains;
Man Knifed; Woman Drowns;
Baby Born Without Face;
Flies Inherit Earth

God says, I have failed.
I say, No way.
I say, You are tops, big guy.
The best.
You gave me
a good wife, good friends,
a place to live . . .
Life is good, I say.
God says, Go to hell, dumbfuck.

The Trial

of a man
accused
of six ax
murders
ended
early today
when the defendant
complained
of a headache.

STEPHEN HICKOFF

Elvis Lives

Brazil rocks.

Yeah, and I'm the Virgin Mary

God is at the back door
of Venus's Fly Trap
with a bottle
and a hard-on . . .

His first woman.

God says, I love you.
I'm God, he says.
And she says: Hey, lover,
we're all somebody.

Eyewitnesses

Man dead—
neighbors say
they were watching television
when they heard the shots.

Avoid Ruin, Ride City

That you must be crippled
to find a parking space
in this world is amazing.

News

Will morning papers arrive?
Imagine headlines—THE END.

Life Signs

Unable to talk to you,
I talk to you.

I scrape my foot along
The stone of you,
The bone of your lip.

Unable to reach for you,
I reach for you.

I taste your sweat
In the soft flesh
Where my arm bends.

Unable to see your face,
I see your face.

I am bending over
The cramp in my side,
Exhaling your breath.

Your death grips me alive.

True Things

Make up the miracles of your life
For me. The true things.
The narrow escapes.
Wasn't it you who went exploring
Caves, got lost and ended up
On a narrow ledge of shale,
The water cold and rising?
You scratched your name, the date,
Into the wall, too terrified
To move. It took a rescue team
Six blessed hours to find the child.

Wasn't it you whose Russian father
The Bolsheviks lined up for execution?
They picked every other man
To shoot. Your father
Watched his brothers fall, crawled
Through mud and slime for miles,
All the way to Detroit and your birth.

And was it you whose violin
Was ardent in his hands?
You who swept down mountains
During World War II, a manic
Sentry saving everyone,
The enemy a continent away?
You who languished in hospital,
Seducing pretty nurses
With your bawdy songs?
You who fished the white waters,
Made broken bulldozers roar,

Ate celery-root salad at midnight,
Your clothes scorched from the fire?

Oh, it was you all along, the miracles
And all the shenanigans.
I bought the whole package.
What did I know?
Breaking promises left and right,
You crashed down dead one fine day,
Leaving me speechless.
Liar. I won't ever believe you again.

The Occupation

Once the professionals had killed one another
and the conscripts had deserted,
the volunteers began to arrive: men who staggered,
eyes merry with wood alcohol,
and sometimes threw away their rifles
because the straps had chafed their shoulders.
We could have killed them, sometimes did,
but there were always more; it was futile
as standing in the rain to sponge the damp
off your old cow's back, or trying to fill out
any of the forms of any of our governments.
These new troops were certain they would die,
giggled over it, only cared about committing
enough crime so that God would not forget them
again in the next world: flies adored them:
even the scavengers who crept after them
barked orders at them; one time
they marched into the next village,
lined up all the livestock against a wall,
and executed them for violation
of an unannounced noon curfew, firing away
until even the hungriest of the scavengers
could only sell the scraps
for lead on the black market.
They came back to our village to apologize.
But by then we were just eyes in the forest,
whispers in an extinct language: we watched
from high in the trees as they dragged out
our old brocade dresses and stuffed them with
      manure,
and bowed down to worship them: they broke

our kitchen chairs for crucifixes:
they knelt in the snow and whipped themselves
with our expensive barbed wire, sobbing
God have mercy, and when they were seriously
    bleeding
and their nude bodies turned sunset colors,
the sergeant slowly shook himself,
took a swig from a private flask,
hitched up his pants, puffed a cigarette
until he stopped shaking, and then barked:
"Eyes right . . . eyes left . . . fall in . . .
attention . . . forward, march."

Liberation

My husband was sentenced to the firing squad
and the poor came and prayed for him
saying, "He was superintendent but so clumsy
at cards, he was almost one of us;
he was a moneylender at interest
but he could never remember when it was
    compounded
and asked us for advice, though we were dying
of hunger, because those were the days
when we adored a painted God, like men
unable to fall asleep, before
the revolution"; and the new authorities
listened, bored, and granted the fool a new life:
instead of coming home, he took advantage
of Liberation to breed his favorite bitch
with one of the landlord's hunting dogs,
and he had to wait there, at the manor,
where it was death to be seen,
until the bitch had her morning sickness,
while he begged the passing troops
for a match for his cold pipe;
when he finally came home, I'd been crying
a solid week, I thought he was resurrected
or just thrown back from death like a runt fish.
I said, "Give me back my week of mourning,
if you have the power to refuse heaven."

The Marriage to War

I always expected my husband to leave me,
because he was the meekest man conceivable.
He sold his fruit trees for my singing lessons,
the quince for the major scales,
the plum for the minor;
then he had to barter his dusty flax
for my arpeggios, and to make weight
he hosed the consignment down.
They caught him, and while he was in prison,
I learned my first recitative
and all of an aria except for one high note.
God knows what they did to him,
but when he came back, I sensed he blamed me:
he began signing contracts with vague salesmen
from countries that had already fallen,
shipping his contract timber by rivers
charted only in obsolete lawbooks;
he was ruining himself slyly, as if with a whore,
but just when he was free, so deep in debt
he held the whole town in the grip of his weakness,
and his worst enemies prayed he would live forever,
the scouts began drifting in from the East:
they built a fire in our rose garden
and pounded on our door, demanding dry kindling;
they surfaced in the market on Sunday
and insisted on paying for every grain of barley,
but the face on their tender had been inked out;
they were only the forerunners of the vanguard,
gorged on the endless dales of Karelia,
and what scared me was the camp followers

still a thousand miles behind: but I changed my
    mind
when I found a buck private hidden
in the coal scuttle, listening to my scales.
When I threatened him with the poker, he shook
    himself
like a dog and whispered, *do re mi, mi re do,*
as if it were a language: then I knew it was time.
I caught my husband as he was drifting out the
    door,
flat paper roses in his pocket, claiming
he was on his way to feed the pond carp,
and I forced him to load our wagon
with the chest of old love letters, the washboard,
the metronome, and a change of linen.
Looking back an hour later, my husband pointed
to a small white cloud and said, "That's our
    house—
if it were wet smoke from green forest wood,
it would have hung in the wind a few seconds
    longer."

Spies

When we stepped into the clearing,
the officers arrested us.
They told us we were pretending
to be afraid, to be homeless,
to be nameless.
They stripped us of disguises.
They shot our horse.
They forced us to speak an unknown language.
They made us swear we were spies
by the blood of Jesus, by our mothers' eyes,
by the smell of bread and mown grass,
by the murmur of a child asleep.
Then they took us to their fortress.

Expulsion

They asked our names, if we were married,
and who were we? They allowed us
to answer the last question with the first two.
Under our breath we were rehearsing: No,
we do not sympathize with the revolution,
the counter-revolution, God, Satan,
or atheism: but they did not ask,
they spared us.
                    It was almost cruel.
Then we stood in the stunning cold
to wait for our visas, in that crowd
of ministers, peddlers, bankers,
judges, thieves, and nuns
huddled outside the garrison door.

GEORGE FRANKLIN

At the Rokkō Hotel

Cutting her husband's
   toenails, the young wife pauses—
      she has a lover.

Frederick II Converses with a Heretic, A.D. *1228*

Whether I myself believe is of
no importance. What counts, my friend,
is power, which you simply don't have.
Please, help yourself to the wine and roast.
After all, tomorrow the offer can hardly
be repeated. But I'm being indelicate.
You'll have to pardon my sense of humor.
I haven't quite recovered from that last
Crusade—the fever, you know.
By God, you *are* an impertinent fellow.
But you're right, of course. I never did
intend to make a go of it. Even His Holiness
caught on to that one. I suppose
I'll have to do it someday, though—
prove I'm not a complete apostate.
Ha! One heretic to another, it's true,
we do live in wretched times. There now,
you see, a few more drinks and you'll
have made a Cathar out of me as well.
But seriously, have you ever seen
a man being burned alive? It's only
the first few minutes that are hard on *him*.
Afterwards, it's the spectators who
have to hold their noses. (You should see
how a priest'll jump back when the stomach bursts.)
Yes, I'm afraid I attend them with rather
disturbing regularity. It's such an
inexpensive way to please the Church.
(Gregory writes me that no other incense
is so preferred by Heaven.) Oh, Lord,
I hadn't realized the time. I must

be off. The ladies in my seraglio
will be wondering what I'm up to. But really,
enjoy your dinner, and make sure you
try the sauce. My chef is quite proud of it.

Lazarus

At first, I squinted, the light burning my eyes,
which were dry and sore and stiff to move.
The shroud had stuck to my skin in places and
hurt as it was peeled back. I tasted wine
from a rag placed upon my lips.

Later, it surprised me that no one, not even
he, asked questions, but I volunteered nothing.
Had someone asked, I could not have answered
    anyway.
I had seen nothing, and there was nothing to see.
No dreams. No visions. Whether it was for a minute
or for a hundred years didn't matter. I had been
    dead.

And though I was grateful to the one who raised
    me,
I had no wish to follow him. For what I had *not*
    seen
had itself become my vision. There would be no
Kingdom of Heaven, and nothing would be eternal
but oblivion, which is always unknown to us.

As for my days now, they are much as they were
before. Only occasionally do I feel a numbness
in the middle of my body and ask my wife to rub
warm olive oil on my chest and back. At such times,
this is all that is real to me: the smell of ripe
olives and her strong hands rubbing in circles
against my heart.

Dido and Aeneas

His cloak was mud-splattered and stiff
and smelled of damp fur, of sweat
and burning wood and the blood of a ewe
sacrificed that morning. He wrapped me
inside of it, saying nothing, staring,
his eyes opaque as a statue's. I should
have turned away from him then, called
to my women or to the leash men
blowing their horns on the far side
of the ridge. I could hear the dogs
breaking through briars and underbrush,
chasing across the open, careless
of scent and quarry, simply eager
to return to the warm hall and fire,
to the tables heavy with game. I should
have gone with them and watched the steam
rise from their coats in the hearth light
and never felt his hands deep beneath
my robe or his black beard pressed
against my thighs. But I had no islands
to wander to, no tribes to conquer,
no prophecies to aid me. In the wet
darkness, there was only his skin
and mouth and the knowing, corrupt
laughter of his gods.

Exploring the Arctic

The Renaissance painters discovered perspective—
That parallel lines appear to meet
At that distant point where vision fails.
On the ice, Peary must never
Have dared to look back.
The sled tracks would have been too much
For any man.
Barrenness is only bearable
If somewhere it ends in a tree or a valley,
One spot not quite erased by the hard
Knife of snow and the infinite cold.
Is there any limit to how cold
A world can be?
Dogs jog painfully along a path
Cut by the compass.
From far away they appear as small
Flecks of iron
Drawn inexorably toward the pole.

Remembrance

The eminent writer, who
recently committed suicide,
discourses on the Holocaust,
which he survived.

As he speaks, slowly,
precisely, the camera plays
back the familiar scenes:
anguished faces; soft piles
of hair; naked bodies pushed
into the pit by bulldozers.

He is riding a bus, being
interviewed as he passes from
one camp to another. He is
sensitive and low-key. Intelligence
shines from his refined face; his
lucidity and dispassion reflect
his training in science.

It is spring as he suffers
this journey. The scenery,
serving as backdrop through the
bus window, is lovely, starting
to be lush, and the segments
that depict him, having been
shot in color, richly contrast
with the grainy quality of the
old footage.

The Life You Did Not Lead

There's a swimming pool.
A breeze ripples the surface.
Dusk. The sky glows, still
fringed with light.

Stars are beginning to
wink on.

Across the valley, a dog
barks, setting off another.

The dogs fall silent.

Now there are crickets.

A slight stir, followed
by murmurs; someone is
refilling the glasses.

You lean back.

Swallows skim the glimmer;
flitter and wheel, difficult
to distinguish from the bats.

Circle and dip and dart.

Double-Dating with Goose

Well, he was smart.
He understood his role.
He'd tell girls flat, I'm everything
you were ever
warned about in Driver Ed.
I drink and smoke and show
off in intersections,
race trains, do doughnuts,
and refuse to yield
the right-of-way.
I'm a son of a bitch at the wheel
and seldom in touch
with reality.

Well, the girls would start
screaming and begging him to stop,
but Goose was off,
blown into one of those crazy moods
to which he was prone,
what with homegrown and malt
and females pretending to be helpless,
so it all added up
to burying the speedometer
in the scream of the road,
beating a lucky guess
through Five Mile Corner
and yelping out of the window
like he was calling to the moon.

Eventually, he'd stop, pull
off roadside, and want to know

what all the fuss was about,
and the girls would say, you're
crazy crazy crazy,
and we're getting out so we
can live awhile longer.
And Goose would sadden and promise,
really promise, to drive like he cared.
Because he was wrong and sorry
and his sister was all crippled and
lived in a wheelchair and could
only put picture puzzles into whole pictures.

So they'd feel something sorry and stay
and he'd kick it
back into gear and tear ninety
toward Columbus, following
Highway 7 toward the horizon line,
laughing and laughing like he was
crazy crazy crazy,
and they'd cry, pounding
on his arm,
you promised you wouldn't,
you promised.

The Dupe

You find Babe's bat in a flea market,
authenticated by a reliable source
and priced right, an extravagance
you can afford.
You hang it
on the wall at home,
holding it in times of crisis.

Even though your game
was never baseball,
you wax your hands
along its sanded grip,
gradually gaining control of the moment,
clenching your fingers
for the shot,
the one that Ruth called
after two strikes

and put

exactly over the wall
where he had pointed.

The Shovel

[1]

1970 was the year I
searched for God, but
found Thoreau instead,

of course, I'd read the
books: Walden, parts of the Bible, a few
lines of the Upanishads, all of Hesse,
and walked the banks of local strip

mines, measuring the
penetration of cattails
into desolated

shores. Considering rebirth
as a theme equal
to simplicity and independence,

I found myself wanting to be another Henry,
skipping out on Nixon, miniskirts, and the Catholic
    church,
walking naked through the woods,
spreading the word as well as I could spell it,
but responding to such free
air exhilaration with an
erection, rather than with

probing insights.

[11]

Charlotte lived in
her parents' white bungalow
on 33rd Street.

On weekends she baby-sat her
brothers, sister, and two
neighbor kids. When I arrived,

heated like a July sidewalk,
she escorted them out
of the house and locked the door.

I never mentioned Thoreau or God,

and we left the TV on, beginning
with Uncle Jed's clog and ending
when Granny chased

Jethro from the kitchen, all the while
threatening to take Elly May
from the banks of the cement pond

and back to the hills
where a girl could grow up
civilized and safe, and away
from the likes of movie producers.

[111]

Today, I take my daughters
to see The Shovel, the gargantuan crank

that stripped Kansas
of coal, mounding rows of
slag and unloading

valleys of topsoil with its truck-sized bucket,
the empty craters
seeping with rain,
leaving the earth to the whims
of wind and sun.

We climb through The Shovel's
wire stripped guts, finger instrument dials
and pull empty levers in the glassy-eyed cab.

We trudge the steps
to the top of the boom
where the same wind that whips the earth
whips our faces and tugs our clothes
like heavy water.
From this height we can see the turned earth,
the section-long trenches
and miles of dumps, the product of hungry men,

who, in their communion
with nature, grew exuberant
and pushed heavy shovels

into the soft soil,
rooting between Charlotte's thighs
like boys.

I Can't Put My Crotch Out

it is burning
out of control
broken out
because nothing
wet
has fallen
on the area
people are saying
to just
cool it
with a spray
but it's spreading
into other areas
with nothing to
stop it
it's time
to take
a rash
act

Foot to Gas

this bus of mine
is trailing
all the others
empty
banged up
jerking
for nothing
braking
for nothing
while the others
shine
full
passing us
like it was
nothing
picking up
everyone

if only
I could get
to the gas

Questions of Need

who needs
to change
bloody sheets

who needs
to give up
a whole bed

who needs
to know someone
more and more

who needs
to have
saliva all over you

who needs
it

Sex

even though
it looks like
that is
exactly
all I am
looking for
and I am
looking for
exactly that
it is
not all
that I am
looking for
exactly

Underground

We both got black diphtheria in 1909,
but Emma, who was nine and already a saint,
was the one God took,
because, Ma said, God takes the good.
I was six, with the Devil in me,
too strong already to die.

I was in my bed by Emma's,
stripped bare and cool as my broken fever,
while they had her service;
"Rock of Ages" pulsed up through the floor,
beating like a heart, the whole
heart of the house downstairs, squeezing
itself around that coffin until
the beating stopped

and my uncles carried it out,
six big men crowded around
to hold the curlicue brass handles of a jewel box.

I watched from my window.

Someone said Emma looked pretty, her hair in
curls, and I remembered
how Emma had wanted my curls
mornings when Ma brushed them one by one
around her first finger
until they wound down in fat links.

Ma remembered, too.
After Emma died and I got well,

every morning stiff bristles dug tracks
in my scalp, and she pulled my curls
into long straight ropes,
weighing them down with her
heavy hands, pulling strand over
strand like despair
crossing in and out of rage,
braiding my hair so tight
that my face stretched taut
across my mind and hurt all day

until I could undo it.
At bedtime, I would sit on Emma's bed
and unbraid myself into the shame and joy
of how the curls sprang back to life,
like something underground pushing up
through the earth,
determined to live
whether it deserved to or not.

Reunion, with White Zinfandel

Look what I have brought you:
the grape skins were left in
just long enough to raise
the faintest blush in the wine,
like a bottle of an unopened dawn,
or a swan eye that remembers us

in the suburbs at eighteen,
our necks fragile and curving
in the early blush of time,
waiting on the station platform
for the New York train
that would take us away.

After my car has spilled
the litter of miles, the children will
spar and laugh through dinner, until
finally, we fold them away
and open the bottle. I will swear
your eyes are no different now;
I will swear we still have time.

In the late cold hours
we will each climb drunkenly
into the beds where
husbands of twenty years snore.
Our coming will stir the sheets
of their sleep to a jagged man-breathing,
but I, for one, will lie
stone-quiet until he is still again,

and run my hands up
and down my body,
thinking it's not so different
as it was: I will wait
on this platform for a train
even as soberness overtakes me,
even as I know
the children will call me
in the first blush light
of their day.

for Susan M. Petrie

Like Any Woman: Those Dreams

Like any woman, I have those dreams
of swinging my headlights a half-moon
away from the house. Last night
I dreamed the rain
and the fog mirrored the lights back
and I forgot not to blink,
not to flinch a look
over my shoulder, where

they stood, where they always stand,
behind the glass door,
hands and faces pressed there,
silent and moist as roses. Their lips
were set like cracks across
the glass but the rain
slid down their faces in murmurs
(we know you, we own you),

in streams, eroding me
like the flow of blood
and love, or something like it,
the murmur I hear like rain:
We know you. We own you.

Ode to a Refrigerator

We trusted you to keep the butter hard
and yet now you murder small, inquisitive children.
Is it any wonder we keep you in chains?
You are obsolete
and obviously very bitter about it.
Sulking alone in our back yard, you are tolerated
because we are lazy. But here is a piece
of news for you:
One more kid and you can kiss your door
goodbye!

Cataclysm

Chicken pox;
Love;
Heart disease.
Things that happen once.

She had something important
she had to tell me.

The earth stood still.
My head spun.

Activities

Sit in subway stations.
Sit by the trash in the park.
Look at Saks Fifth Avenue.
Look at Tchelitchev.
Think about the past.
Go to a McDonald's and kill everybody.
Vote for President.
Read a small-business networking catalogue
         until 4 A.M.
Fall in love.
Stare at the sun.
Get back up.
Eat a whole bunch of baked potatoes.

B-Minor Mass

What could we want from Johann Sebastian
but to slow down for the Crucifixion,
then raise the roof with Jesus Risen?
That melodrama was a way of telling
what music would have us take from mystery
before we came to find out otherwise—
stopping where faith begins, bringing the truth
down from among those rafters rent with song.
I keep on hearing something else again,
the Crucifixion's joy, the Rising's terror,
Nature's relentless will to do us harm,
then leave us humming snatches of a tune
we lost the words for, while the morning light
sang from above to taunt us as we mourned.

Texas

I told her I was from Texas
Because I didn't like the way
She looked at me
The tone of her voice
The way she wore
Her dress
She was from
New York
Tokyo
Paris
Milan
I told her I was from Texas
And smiled
Good word:
Texas
Pronounced right
Sounds a lot like
Fuck you

I Want to Write You Long Letters

I want to write you long letters
Tell you everything
I want to tell you how it rained in Georgia
I want to tell you about bus stations
And the coughing
Of the lower classes
I want to write you long letters
Put my cards on the table
I want to clear the air
Explain myself
The context
The circumstances
I want to write you long letters
Tell you everything
I want to be funny
I want to write you long letters
Describe to you America
I want to tell you about America
About the water pressure in America
About porcelain
And the gravel shoulders
I want to write you long letters
Let you see what I see
The tired houses
That sit shaded and snug
Chairs on the porch
Ivy up the sides
The paint worn from the stairs
The banisters bent and falling
I want you to see what I see
The way the wind beats down

The rain beats down
The skies beat down
And everything burns
I want you to see what I see
I want you to understand
I want to write you long letters
I want you
To know

Cutting Hair

I used to stand useless
near a corner of her bathroom
while she spread newspapers on the floor.
She wanted my hair wet and left me
as I bent beneath the faucet,
waiting elsewhere until I'd rubbed
the water through,
held the mass of brown in her fresh towel,
then walked the papers
to the center of the room. I kept
my glasses off.
A trim was all I ever asked for.
I wanted the blunt edge
her mother cut for her, the silky broom
her hair formed on her back.

She cut a splinter at a time.
I felt dizziness rise
as I stared at the smudge of room
and listened to my voice, the rasp
of her scissors, and the dry slap of water drops
as they struck a page.
She wasn't afraid she'd cut off more
than I had wanted—she never asked if I was
    pleased.
It was just that the job was hers.
I always folded up the newspapers
too fast and had to stand and watch
her put her tools away.
She wouldn't use the comb I'd bring.

She never let me cut her hair.
And all those times I kept coming back
to her, offering secrets in trade
as she bent and circled me.
All I wanted was
for her to put the scissors in my hand
and close her eyes.

After the Day

How long did you say
it would take for you
to have a nuclear dream?
Things falling from
the sky, even the sky itself.
Pieces of atmosphere big
enough to trip over.

I call my mother
in Chicago. The phone rings
ten times. Ninety-nine
miles for every ring.
Glass in her hair
blends with the gray.

First, my hair
comes out in strands. Embedded
in my palm. New lifelines
to knot and braid. My mouth
is an open sore. I leave
fingerprints on my scalp.

Poem

Her letter arrived today
with drawings on the outside looking more like
    atomic mushroom clouds
than the flowers
they were intended
to be.

It was the same on the inside.

Poem

The fact
that I read
her stupid fucking horoscope every goddamned day
    must prove
that I
still love her.

Stamps

In my hand there are two American stamps.
As of today it costs
twenty-five cents to mail a letter.
These stamps are no longer effective.
They are three cents short.
If I wanted to mail two letters,
I'd need six one-cent stamps.

This is how I feel
about her
now.

Poem

She called at 1:41 A.M.
and let it ring twice,
knowing that in two I wouldn't be able to get it.
I haven't heard the sound of her voice
once in seven months
and she lets it ring twice.

After it rang,
I picked it up to hear a dial tone
that was unmistakably hers.

Spider

I caught a spider sucking a drink
From the kitchen sponge. Its thirst
Disgusted me. I didn't want to know
How our requirements coincide.
Still, the spider was almost beautiful
As it stepped from the wet sponge
And swung into the pot of mint,
Where I knew
It would rest and hide and savor
The cool taste of water
In its dark mouth.

Crab

Before dying, the old woman became crab-
like. Her spotted hand backs became
algae-emeralded. "How pretty I
am!" she said. But her big
toe, with its violet spur
of crimped nail, clicked
in pincer snips, and she
screamed. Only her soft
mouth that had loved to suck
oysters and grapes amazed
her with its red machinery
of appetite. I saw her slow
serene eyes shinny up their
stems.
        A crab, and sunset-
crimson as a crab, her hunched
belly glittered. Only in her
bath was there still
that drowned flower of helplessness.
I watched her scuttle breathing
sideways to say "How pretty
I am." I hated
her crabbedness, even while I comforted
the alert pinnacles where her grieving
eyes began. But "Nobody
can forgive
you now," she
hissed.

Lichens

Between the stones, by the sea's edge,
And in sheltered hollows of the rock,
Flat lichens cling. Their surfaces are gray,
Dry, and crinkly. Some are cracked and sharp
Or flake away like weathered paint in strips.
They survive the cold light and the spray
Torn from the North Atlantic. The way they clasp
And cover the rocks seems to signify
Inconspicuous courage and tenacity. But
At evening they gleam bleakly in exact
Configurations and their order is fiercer
Than the seas: their drab arabesques
Look splotchy, rust-wept, or scaly as dead bark;
Far off, they're starlike, spiky as galaxies.
Like us they clutch and grip their chilly homes
And the wind defines their possibilities.

The Theory of Everything

[1]
There is a God.

He wants a flower the size of Philadelphia
    to open in the moonlight
even when the moonlight
    is dirty.

The universe is something I can believe in.
It can't be defined by roundness

it folds into darknesses dragging currents
that breathe   it sucks back into

itself.

All the mothers and fathers of the night sitting
    bedside
outside windows, behind scratchy jukeboxes,

liquor oozes down multiple throats

soars into the back steps of wooden apart-
ments—staring strangely at the moon

—the moon listens and breathes

    into houses—

        taking responsibility

for the sad kisses, the broken windows.

[11]

Charlie, jazz is everything

I ever wanted:
    An everything; it includes
    a never-leaving, it holds
    the notes
    even in silence.

[111]

The overlapping hands of the ten dimensions are
    impossible to comprehend.
I can't even envision:
    the light from each broken star that hides

the mother the father

the indiscriminate lovers—
    A straight line they can walk across
    A second line perpendicular
    The place jazz passes

where light does not exist.
    How fire parts air and slips

into the past,   how fire exists
    in the leaving—
    A porch door swinging
    An empty house   where everything is a dark
        bird singing—

The father the mother come together to *stay,*
    they say:

We want to leave the door open he was playing *so*
pretty.

    for Charlie Parker

Clink into the Arms of America

Measure emptiness by the plate glass smashed,
she said to herself, forget the coffee,
out loud. Fucking mother, what am I, gashed
across America, can't you see? Sloppy
is my trail, naked and run-down. Hoping
for those dark eyes, I search mine fields blank,
    wrong.
There's a cactus in my heart exploding
with the storm clouds. I simply have no song,
Lord! I destroy the tune for any house.
Jam-packed w/ nicotine fingers, I fight
the jagged edges. I strip the fat grouse
wingless, I rip them, guiltless, from their flight.

I'm a target for the interruption.
I'm a shotgun silencing discussion.

Self-Portrait as the Idea Between Them

The ocean hushes this gesture

to the clay cliffs eroding

to become more than this idea

which imagines itself to be

spreading clay all over itself

to become bigger than all this

distance

the sound of the only window to you is drifting
keeps drifting

Frozen Rope

I'm in the 3 Rivers parking lot
and Al Oliver's holding my baseball in his hand.
My ball.
He's using it to make a point.
He's telling some guy in a wool sweater
how a man can't have his privacy.
I'm eight, but I've had all I can take.
Al, I say.
Do me a favor.
Sign the ball
the way I sign your paychecks.
That's right, me.
Dom Leone, eight.
Then go in there and hit the ball
like you always do.
On a hard line, deep,
and to the opposite field.

The Jesus for Dom

Aw, I can't do anything right.
    For example, sometimes it still rains,

And that guy over there,
    I think he needs glasses.

While She Sleeps

If I could hurl backyard apples
beyond city lights, would you hear
them knuckle down your roof
like a hand tapping at your chest?

And if my arms could sway like branches,
would you feel them lean across town,
lift you from your bed and ease you
down through the trees, wind still rustling
the flannel of your gown?

By the time I eased you back,
school children would be racing
beneath my arms, your heart
tapping out its small buds,
a river of yellow roses.

July 19th

Called my dad long distance,
7:45 AM, my coffeepot sputtering
up vowels of oxygen. He was out there,
not some voice to drag down
from the sky, piece together with prayer,
like a drunken man, arms and legs wrapped around
a telephone pole, whispering to a spot
gouged out by a car bumper,
glad to not be alone.

He felt that if
it wasn't easy,
it wasn't right

When I last wrote, I was on my way to Disneyland with my friend, who is dying. There are horrible parts to it, of course. But what most people don't say is that there is something exciting about someone dying. It galvanizes everything; it brings one's noblest (and probably most deluded) sense of oneself rushing to the surface. You think that you will prove just how self-sacrificing you can be. Too, there's a sense that something important will be said once there is nothing left to lose. This is the subtext to the drama of the hospital visits and the doctor visits and the great fear. It works well before the person begins to lose energy or get disfigured or starts to smell. Until then, it doesn't seem as if anything is really happening. You think this isn't so bad, considering it's the biggest thing that ever happened to you. After the first shock, you've still got to buy groceries and pick up your dry cleaning. It seems to you that it could go on okay this way forever. So you are able to have your thoughts about dying in someone's arms. You know, like Huxley's wife shooting him full of acid and whispering, "Go toward the light." I guess I saw Disneyland as a sort of prelude to this. It is not the place I would have chosen. But since my friend did, I thought, Well, he'll speak wistfully of it as he draws his last breath, and I'll feel virtuous that I took him there and gave him his last wish, even if it might have been a better one. Forget it. The place was a total horror. It makes you feel as if you have no business being out in the world. The people there are absolutely terrifying. I don't really see things in terms of sexual division, but there were only two other people that one could see were homosexuals, and they looked scared silly. That's how I felt, anyway. My friend loved it. We waited in line for hours to see Frontierland, to go on Star Wars rides. He even bought hideous glass mugs with our names engraved under Mickey Mouse's feet while I snuck off to smoke a cigarette. His favorite ride was this thing called It's a Small World, little boats that take you through a canal in this cavernous place—really endless—lit with lurid neon lights. All along the sides are painted mechanical dolls—little Chinese dolls, Injun dolls, African dolls, penguins, ducks, monkeys; I swear, there were even Filipino dolls—with moving mouths. They sway and wave with their little hands as your boat passes. All the while, a canned recording of a song ("It's a Small World, After All") blares out over and over again through a tinny loudspeaker—deafening. It takes about fifteen minutes to get past all the continents. Did I say there were Eskimos, Polynesian girls, Dutch maidens, midgets in kilts? I think even a couple of cows. I turned to my friend to say, "I'm going to throw myself into the water if this doesn't end soon," and saw that he was looking at this international nausea with misty eyes, tapping his foot to the terrible song. It crossed my mind that it must be natural to get sentimental if you think you're about to go. He made me ride through it two more times. Then off we went to Sea World to pet the dolphins—which, secretly, I liked doing. But the same people who were at Disneyland clearly had got on the next bus for San Diego, because they were everywhere.

By the time we got to Sea World, it seemed more as if he was dying. He couldn't hear. He had a pain in his ear so severe that he wept. He had no energy. His voice was changing to this weird whisper, the way somebody speaks after he's just vomited. It all came on overnight. He had had eczema for years—all over his body—and suddenly one night, months ago, it went away. It vanished when no treatment had hitherto made any difference. This fed the notion of all that bullshit about mind over body; a good attitude, you can will yourself to be alive. I've always believed in my heart that the body is our enemy. Anyway, he said the eczema had gone away because he was so happy. It did seem rather miraculous. But at Sea World, the scales sprang back with a vengeance, bubbles everywhere on his skin spreading as we walked. He had on the sort of T-shirt where one can see the back and chest, so I could tell it was everywhere. I couldn't look at anything else, of course. When we went to our hotel, all we did was stare at his skin. I thought, He hates me—because the spots mean some sort of emotional change. In fact, he did turn on me. Immediately. "Can't see you anymore," he said. When I asked why, he said it was because he couldn't forgive the horrible things that I had been saying about him behind his back. He would not sit with me on the airplane home. I spent the trip tallying every dime I had spent—I couldn't stop myself. It was thousands. He has no money left. He jumped into a cab the minute we arrived. Two days later, there was a note from him on my desk, along with the mug from Disneyland, the one with my name on it, and seven dollars. **Q**

XMAS SHOPPING with PENA

NORMALLY A MODEL OF SELF-CONTROL, PENA
ALLOWED HERSELF THIS ONE IMPULSE-ITEM.

IT WAS NOT HER UNRELIEVED LONELINESS OR
IMPENDING FINANCIAL DISASTER, THE NOTE
SAID, BUT THE REAPPEARANCE OF SLUGS IN
HER BACK GARDEN.

IN HER DREAM, RAGS HAD FAILED OBEDIENCE-
TRAINING AND ROLF HAD SETTLED ON WHAT
HE CALLED "THE FINAL SOLUTION."

CERTAIN EVENTS IN DEE-DEE'S CHILDHOOD PREVENTED HER FROM LETTING GO OF HERB'S LEG.

HAROLD WAS CONVINCED THAT HIS DEPRESSION SPRANG FROM A TIME OF MATERNAL DEPRIVATION.

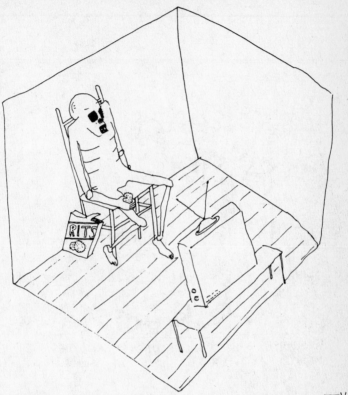

DEATH EATING CRACKERS AND WATCHING T.V.

TO THOSE WHO DID NOT UNDERSTAND, LEDA
WOULD ANSWER, "HE'S HUMAN AND HE'S
MINE."

HAPPILY, GEORGE COULD SPEND NIGHT AFTER NIGHT WITH HIS HINDEMITH.

The Woman Who Knew Too Much

ALFRED'S SILENCE COULD BE EXPERTLY DECODED:
"I LOVE YOU, DARLING, MORE THAN LIFE ITSELF" WAS
WHAT IT MEANT.

THE WOMAN WHO HAD IT ALL

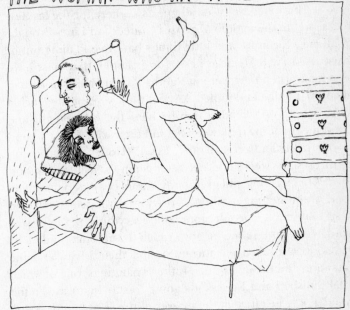

THE TIME WAS 7:00, THE SHOW WAS "JEOPARDY," AND THE CATEGORY WAS "EATING HABITS OF THE STARS."

I have had wall-to-wall guests up here for the last few weeks, and in the middle of all this United Van Lines brought up Mama's furniture and little things have been falling out of drawers—a 1978 Mexican peso, for example, that must have been from when they were in Puerto Vallarta and Daddy had taken the pledge and joined AA and they were having such a good time. Two friends came by here the other night and found me up at my desk weeping and they said, "That's good for you, to cry and get it all out." I said, "Honey, I been crying for three solid weeks and my sister Sunny's been crying and Roger's been crying and everybody's been crying, so don't talk to me about getting it all out." Anyway, I wanted to have all these visitors and people gone and everything peaceful so I could write and sound happy, which I am, surrounded by Mama's beautiful maple furniture, and their silver, and the glassware, and the linen, and Mother's paintings, one of which is half finished and I guess it's going to stay that way. Found an old 3 × 4 negative in the drawer of the secretary desk and had it printed, and it turns out it's Maxie Belle, about age sixteen, wearing Daddy's navy uniform and looking as beautiful as a movie heroine—Rosie the Riveter, Seaman First-Class. The house is the old yellow house in Salem where I was born. We went in to start clearing out Mama's house before the funeral, and found Nettie had come in and cleaned it from one end to the other and set out flowers. She said she wanted to do it for Ruby. It was about 102°, and I thought, The men are going to expire in those suits in the church. And we were all determined not to Break Down, because people were coming with food and expressing regrets and everything, and they're supposed to Break Down, not you. Then Maxie found my baby book. Mama used to write in our baby books like they were

novels, all up the side of the page when she ran out of room. Maxie sat down at the table and started crying like a rainstorm, and I know what it was, I know the page exactly: it was where Mama wrote about Maxie coming by with a new dress for me and to take me out walking when I was four. Then Sunny got hold of herself by saying it looked like she'd lost Skippy's arms for good. Skippy was this little porcelain doll Mama kept since she was eight; Skippy was some kind of comic-book character from the thirties, and you could get a Skippy doll from an oatmeal box. Maxie said an old fellow down in Lynn Creek gave her one and Mama one, but Maxie lost hers, or traded it, and eventually Mama's didn't have any arms, but she held onto that doll through everything. I don't know why. Sunny values it very much and she's going to put it in the old walnut cabinet along with the silver cup Mama won for singing in sixth grade. I thought, I know where those arms are, and I went and looked in the drawer of the night table, and there they were, along with Daddy's Kansas City Life cigarette lighters and stuff. So I took them in to her, and said, "Shine, look here." And Sunny LEAPED to her feet and grabbed them and yelled, "YOU FOUND SKIPPY'S ARMS!" and she burst into tears with one arm in each hand, and started shaking, and kept yelling, "YOU FOUND SKIPPY'S ARMS!" as if he had been snatched miraculously out of the grave-hole, and if he hadn't of had his arms we wouldn't have saved him, he'd have gone down too. Well, you got to save somebody. Then Aunt Mayme nearly collapsed when she saw Mama at the funeral. I didn't look. I had my eye on my brother, wondering if he'd get violent again anyway. It gave me something to think about and get mad about, to keep from crying. He managed to kind of borrow three thousand dollars off Mama when she was living on Social Security and going to that damn charity hospital so as not to be a burden. He talks her out of three thousand dollars, and he's had a steady job at the Salada Salad Dressing plant for twenty-five years and is a member of the Teamsters. You'd think he could have managed to borrow it from the bank. That, and knocking my sister down with his fist for even bringing up the matter, is why Brother Emory kept us separated from him—with him and his lot on one side of the church and us on the other. I tried to get my cousin Raymond to come, as he's with the Sheriff's Department over in Audrain County. But I guess he was too busy arresting people. Then I wanted Hugh Vaughn to come in case of trouble, but Hugh Vaughn won't go to funerals ever since he got back from Vietnam. Anyway, there wasn't any trouble. So I sat there and tried not to look at Mayme crying, thinking, If I lost *my* sister, I'd cry worse than that even, and Sunny held on to my hand with Skippy's arms in her other fist. Brother Emory preached an intelligent and moving sermon about lavender, which was what Mama always used for the shadow colors in her paintings, and he quoted from Joel and Psalms and talked about how families have to stick together, as ours has, with one little exception. Then when they screwed down the coffin lid, my brother burst out crying, bent over with his head in his hand, and I thought, Cry all you want, Rambo, just pay that money back to the estate so we can pay the doctors off. Then we all walked out to the grave behind the coffin. If it was hot in the church with the fans going, it was like being microwaved outside. We sat by the grave. Brother Emory opened up *Blackwater* and read the epigraph. I started kind of groaning. Then it rained. It rained on me right at the graveside, and I put my head on my mother's coffin and cried till I couldn't see straight. Sunny said, "Come on, come on, baby, get on your feet," and Roger patted me on the shoulder. So I did. Then Sunny and I got some of the flowers from the offerings, and put some gladiolas on Great-grandma Nannie Hanlin's grave and some on our little brother's grave, and we went off to our live feuding and our pettiness and left another generation on the hill. Q

WHOOPS...SORRY!   YL

In Defense of Pater

Group Day at .
   The Rhinelander
   was always such
   a trial.

YL

ANOTHER DATE WITH LILIAN

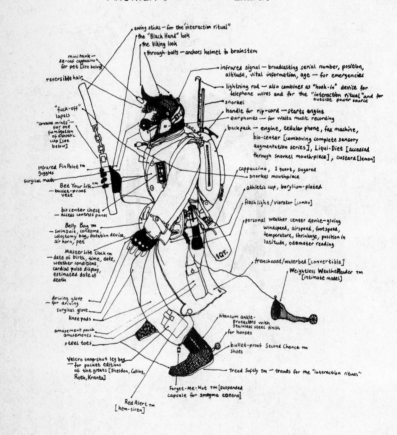

Read the fucking
caption, punk!

My sister Sukey tells me, "You don't sound so good."

I tell her I've been carrying around a prescription for Librium for two weeks.

"Two weeks?" My sister says, "I once carried around a prescription for Clomid for a year."

"The stuff they put in pools?"

"That's good," Sukey says. Her laugh has no build. Neither has mine. It's no surprise. Sukey is more than my older sister. She is my trailblazer. I never needed an abortion until Sukey had hers. She pierced her ears at a time when the only place you saw that was *National Geographic.* Now I think I am waiting for her to get a divorce so I can contemplate one of my own. The more things she does that I wind up doing, the more I sense the inevitability of not doing anything she hasn't already done. I hope she doesn't spike her hair. I would look lousy in spiked hair.

"You're getting too close to yourself," Sukey says. "You have to go do something nice for somebody else and it will get you out of yourself."

"But if I do something nice for somebody else to get me out of myself, aren't I really doing something nice for me?"

"Tell me something. This prescription. Is it for 5's, 10's, or 25's?" my sister Sukey wants to know.

So I think, Hey, I've never been down to Aunt Ida's place. Maybe I should go to see Aunt Ida for the last time. She is the oldest in the family. The oldest sister of my grandmother, the first to go gray, the most bent over, the one with the most body parts removed. The one with the most body parts not even hers. A metal hip. An artery that's 100 percent polyester. The thinnest, the poorest. The one widowed first. A son in small leather goods a coast away. Broken-down clothes from relatives. The only thing Aunt Ida ever had first was gallstones. The only thing she could ever call her own.

I dial her number. I know she will be home because she is recovering from a colostomy.

"Hello?"

"Aunt Ida!"

"Who's this?"

"Patty!"

"Patty who?"

"Patty Volk. Patty Bogen Volk."

"Who?"

"Ethel Melnick's granddaughter. Millie Bogen's daughter. Sukey Glickstein's sister. Randy Volk's wife."

"Sukey! Darling! How are you?"

"*Patty.*"

"Patty! Darling! How's Sukey?"

"Do you feel like a little company?" I ask. This for sure will be the last time. This really feels like *it.* Aunt Ida is eighty-nine and no longer has a large intestine.

"Come for lunch!" Aunt Ida says. "I haven't seen you in a long time, Sukey."

"Patty."

"Bring her too."

I have two hours to kill, so I wash my hair and finger-dry it and put on makeup so I look as if I'm not wearing any and find a bottle of cream sherry for Aunt Ida, and before I know it, I am late. So I take a cab down to a neighborhood that has undergone three ethnic transitions since my great-grandparents first settled there. The thought that I have come down here to console myself by finding a human being more miserable than I am is so awful I have to tell myself I can't help what I think. I have come down here to get myself out of myself and do a good turn. I have come down here to bring cheer and cream sherry to a dying older woman with no bowel and a son in small leather goods.

Aunt Ida's apartment is in a flaking five-story brownstone with a shop on the ground floor that sells trusses, bedpans, and orthopedic shoes. I wonder if there's anything in the store Aunt Ida could use. Maybe the cream sherry is enough. She probably won't have time to finish a whole bottle, anyway.

So I open the street door and buzz up. Since she lives on the top floor, her button is on the bottom, beneath Chang, Gonzales, and Marmelst (Marmelstein, if the name tag had been long enough). Aunt Ida's button is the cleanest. So she's having visitors. That's good. Everyone is coming to see Aunt Ida for the last time. Suddenly I realize I should have brought food. Aunt Ida has no money. Aunt Ida can't go out. Aunt Ida is starving. I despise myself for not thinking of it. Food! The money I spent on taking a cab down here could have kept Aunt Ida in Beech-Nut baby food and mashed bananas for a week.

Aunt Ida doesn't answer my buzz, so I hit Chang, Gonzales, and Marmelst, and pretty soon I am in. The walls of the entryway are tiled in yellow, and like all small dark places in the city—the phone booths, service elevators, even the back seats of cabs—it smells like men's piss. Sometimes I think that if I didn't know that smell was men's piss, if it was, say, the smell of a flower, I'd like it.

I start up the stairs, trying to balance myself. There is no banister and the walls lean in, so that the higher you go, the harder your body is pressed into them. They are mustard-colored stucco covered in grease. How could my family let Aunt Ida live like this?

I bang on the door and finally shout, "It's me, Aunt Ida, Patty! Let me in!"

Nothing.

I bang harder. "Anybody home?" I shout. Maybe the excitement from my buzzing did her in.

Then the police bolt jolts out of the floor. A lock unclicks. A sweet-looking black girl probes me through the gap.

"Who is it, Catherine?" I hear Aunt Ida holler.

"I'm her niece," I say conspiratorially, as if to say, You know how the old are. "She's expecting me."

"She says she's your niece," Catherine hollers back. Silence.

"Tell her it's Patty Bogen Volk, please," I say.

Catherine opens the door, keeping her body behind it, and, quite suddenly I am plunged into my youth. Here is the coffee table with the peeling gold-leaf legs that graced my mother's living room when I was growing up, the floor lamp from my grandmother's with the inverted green leather shade that provided light only for the ceiling, the pink convertible sofa that was considered by three generations to be my mother's single most serious consumer error, and the red-and-blue Oriental rug we gave away when we gave away the dog that ruined it.

"Get my niece a chair, Caroline," Aunt Ida says, coming out of the bedroom.

It looks to me as if there is no bulge where the bag is.

"You know what they did to me?" Aunt Ida grabs my arm.

"I can't believe how good you look, Aunt Ida," I say. For the first time, I have to bend down to kiss her. This latest round with the doctors has shaved inches off her height.

"My hair," Aunt Ida says. "You like my hair?"

"How do you do it?" I marvel. Her hair does, in fact, look perfect. "I mean, really."

"Come," she nudges. "I made you lunch."

"Aunt Ida! You're supposed to be taking it easy!"

"I didn't do it. Cynthia did it." She nods to Cynthia and Cynthia beams and twists her calves around each other.

My father's old collapsible bridge table is covered with Aunt Fay's green felt canasta cloth. Bright pink cut grapefruit lie like jewels on Uncle Harry's first wife's gilt-edged service plates. Aunt Ida is using Grandma's everyday flatware. I realize

227

I have not seen grapefruit spoons since my grandmother died.

I am struck with the notion that nobody will ever take this trouble for me again, that the last time I will see Aunt Ida is also the last time I will see grapefruit spoons.

"Here's some sherry," I tell Aunt Ida. "You always loved cream sherry."

Aunt Ida opens her mouth and nothing comes out. Then, "Cinderella!" she blurts. "The sherry glasses!"

Cinderella brings, oh my God! my grandfather's silver-rimmed sherry glasses, which he used at his Thursday-night bridge game. I am overcome. I wonder if Aunt Ida also has the wall-sized radio with the steering-wheel station selector I used to talk to God on.

Aunt Ida pours half glasses and we clink.

"To health and happiness," she says, and I search her eyes for a double entendre. Does she mean health and happiness for me? For her? For us?

"So tell me, Sukey," she sighs, "what's new?"

Since I haven't seen Aunt Ida in over a year, I don't know whether to tell her that the cleaner lost my favorite blouse yesterday or that actually I'm Patty, not my sister Sukey. What's new? always throws me. Where to start? What's important? Who cares?

"Sukey sends her love," I say.

"Eat!" Aunt Ida is not happy with the progress I am making. In my family, if you haven't ravaged a grapefruit, you haven't enjoyed it. I wonder how many food stamps Aunt Ida sacrificed for an Indian River grapefruit. If it would make her happy, I'd take the zest home for baking and use the oil in the skin for scenting soap.

"So what do you think of my robe?" Aunt Ida asks, flicking a bony hand over the dishes.

Cinderella clears.

"You may bring the main course now, Graziela," Aunt Ida signals with a royal wave.

I say, "Nobody ever wore clothes like you, Aunt Ida. I

mean that." The robe is blue, Aunt Ida's color, and ruffled at the neck and down the front. It stands away from her like clown pants.

Graziela sets the salad down. It is chopped beyond recognition, molded in the center of Aunt Fay's vegetable platter. Aunt Ida dismisses Graziela and serves majestically. It occurs to me that, in many ways, Aunt Ida's never had it so good. Full-time help, a new robe. Where did she get this wonderful food?

"You know who sent me this robe?"

"My mother," I guess.

"Who?" Aunt Ida says.

"Millie Bogen."

"Norman sent me this robe. Norman! Can you imagine? All the way from California! Such a son I have! Nobody, nobody has a son like me!"

She drops some salad on my plate.

"Norman loves you," I say, taking a taste.

"I'm the luckiest woman in the world," Aunt Ida says. "You like the salad?"

"Ummm," I say. It is quite tasty. "What's in it?"

"Guess!" Aunt Ida's blue eyes light up.

"Well, the orange stuff is carrots."

"Carrots, Gracie!" she calls to her companion. "Go on!"

"Chicken?"

"No!"

"Mayonnaise?"

"Hah!"

"Tuna?"

"Hah! Tuna! Stacy! Hah! Hah!"

"I give up," I say, holding up my plate for a second helping. It's absolutely delicious.

"Then you'll never know, will you?"

Oh God. Oh no. It's dog food. It must be dog food. How could she afford anything else?

"Eat!" Aunt Ida encourages me. "It's good for you."

"Please tell me what's in it, Aunt Ida."

"And let you steal my recipe? Fat chance."

Aunt Ida takes a bite and chews it with her front teeth.

"Did it come in a can?" I ask sheepishly.

"I made this recipe up from scratch," Aunt Ida says. "You could never duplicate it even if I gave you the recipe. There is a possibility that even I will never be able to duplicate it. Right, Stephanie?"

"Right, Mrs. Stavin." Stephanie nods.

"Only Selena and I know what went into this salad. Only Selena and I will ever know. Now eat. Don't waste it."

I feel as if eating Aunt Ida's mystery salad is the last kind thing I will ever be able to do for her. Wait till Sukey hears I ate dog food.

"What's in it, Selena?" I ask, turning in my seat. Selena stands behind me so Aunt Ida can catch her eye.

"Don't you tell her, Sabena. I mean it," Aunt Ida says.

"Aw, come on, Sabena. Tell me," I say. I can't believe, with everything my family's done for her, that Aunt Ida won't give me her recipe.

"*No!*" Aunt Ida rises out of her seat and shouts.

Since I don't want to be responsible for giving Aunt Ida her last heart attack, I retreat. I can't believe she would make such a big deal over it. What am I going to do? Sell the recipe for a billion dollars to *Woman's Day*? She's got the best son in the world, the best robe in the world, does she need the best salad recipe in the world too?

A homemade chocolate cake appears. It is so light you can see air through it, light and lofty, almost quivering on—what? My old cake stand! How did Aunt Ida get my old cake stand? When was the last time I saw that cake stand? I used to love that cake stand.

"My Norman calls me every week. He can't wait to talk to me," Aunt Ida says. "He always asks me how I am." Aunt Ida glows. "Always, he says, 'Love ya, Mom,' before he hangs up. 'Love ya.' Just like that. I am blessed. Do you know that?"

"You were a wonderful mother, Aunt Ida. The whole entire family knows how you fed him heavy cream in his cereal
when he was a boy."

"In his cereal! I let him drink it right from the glass."

"Well, a boy doesn't forget that, Aunt Ida."

"I want you to take a piece of cake home. Serena, please,
a Ziploc bag!"

Aunt Ida slips a sliver into the bag.

"Could I have another piece for my husband?" I ask.

"Who's this one for?" Aunt Ida waves the Ziploc.

"I thought we could each have a piece for dessert tonight," I say.

She sticks the knife in the Ziploc and cuts the cake in half.
She looks at me with less than love. I see I have overstepped
the line. I stare back at her, trying to memorize her.

"Hey, Aunt Ida," I say, "remember the time at Grandma's
you taught me how to roll bread balls on the tablecloth and
make my finger feel dead?"

"That's the most disgusting thing I ever heard," she says,
waving Aunt Bessie's cake knife at my heart.

I walk to Aunt Ida's side of the table, and push her arm
away like a turnstile. I hug her to me. Aunt Ida's breasts, if she
still has them, do not come between us. I feel nothing but
billowing air as I try hugging Aunt Ida tighter, getting closer
and closer, waiting to feel the pressure of her colostomy bag
against my hip. Aunt Ida smells as sweet as the talc her sister,
my grandmother, used to keep on top of the toilet tank.

Aunt Ida pushes me back.

"Sabrina, help me to bed. I'm a little tired."

"I'll help you."

"No. I want Sabrina."

Sabrina offers Aunt Ida her arm and then braces Aunt Ida
around the back with her other arm. They walk, locked together like ice skaters, into the bedroom.

I pick a crumb off the cake stand and carry the crumb into
the kitchen. I open the cabinet door beneath the sink. I tip the

garbage pail toward me. It smells medicinal. A few orange and gray carrot scrapings are stuck to the plastic liner bag.

Sabrina comes out of the bedroom looking distracted.

"May I go in and say goodbye?" I ask. Goodbye forever?

"She says to tell you she is resting," Sabrina says. "And to thank you for coming."

"What, exactly, is your name?" I ask Sabrina, adjusting my shoulder bag.

"Elvita," she says, opening the door.

I start to slide out. "And what," I say, as if it's an afterthought, "was in that salad, actually, Elvita?"

"Tofu, honey," she says, closing the door behind me.

Tofu!

Of course!

No.

Wait.

Tofu, *honey*?

Tofu *and* honey?

Or tofu, *honey,* as in *dear*?

Or was it tofu, *honky*?

I call my sister to tell her Aunt Ida's on her last leg.

"She's down to one?" my sister Sukey says.

I take a long shot and ask my sister when she gave Aunt Ida my old cake stand.

"You only like that cake stand because somebody has it."

I tell her about the recipe, how Aunt Ida wouldn't give it to me.

"That's right," my sister Sukey says. "Keep asking people for something. Keep giving them the chance to say no."

"Are you telling me I set myself up? Is that what you're telling me? You think I set myself up?"

"No," my sister Sukey says. "And Liz Taylor never had a face-lift." **Q**

Here's us, bowling in New Jersey. Don't even ask how we got here—I couldn't tell you. I used to bowl when I was a kid. But this wasn't the old *fun* bowling—this was the new *ironic* bowling. **Q**

World Books
18 West 38th St.
NYC 10015

Dec. 19, 1987
102 East 22nd St.
NYC 10010

Dear Sirs:

I have a little explaining to do. I was at World Books yesterday
to buy a book on Egyptian hieglyphics as a Christmas present for my mother, who is planning a trip to Egypt. I found a
suitable book, but the cashier's line was really around the
block, and I was in a major hurry, having left all my shopping
till the last minute as usual.

To make a long story short, I just slipped the book into my
shopping bag and walked out with it. But I never intended to
steal the book. I just couldn't hack the cashier's line right then.
I'm sure you've had those kinds of days.

The price of the book was $17.95. I'm enclosing a check
for $20, which should also cover the tax.

Very truly yours,
Donald M. Shea

TO   : MR. D. SHEE
REF ORDER NO. : 00080766
DATE   : 01/22/88

WE ARE SORRY BUT WE CANNOT FILL YOUR ORDER AS RECEIVED.
WE NEED THE FOLLOWING ADDITIONAL INFORMATION: BOOK
TITLE, AUTHOR, PUBLISHER.

WE ARE ENCLOSING A REFUND CHECK IN THE AMOUNT OF $20.00.
PLEASE REFER TO ORDER NO. 00080766 IN ANY FUTURE CORRE-
SPONDENCE. THANK YOU FOR SHOPPING AT WORLD BOOKS.

World Books
18 West 38th St.
NYC 10015

Jan. 26, 1988
102 East 22nd St.
NYC 10010

Hey guys, anyone home? I thought I was pretty clear the first time, but let's try again.

Order No. 00080766 is not an order. I stole a book from your store at Christmas because I didn't want to wait in line to pay for it. I'm trying to pay for it now.

The book is *An Introduction to Hieroglyphics* by James Harris, Columbia University Press, 1984. I enclose yet another check for $20.00.

Walking out with the book like that was a regrettable impulse. I should have been more patient. I'd like to get it off my mind.

By the way, my last name is spelled Shea, not Shee.

Hopefully yours,
Don Shea

TO   : MR. D. SHEE
REF ORDER NO. : 00080766
DATE   : 02/18/88

WE ARE SORRY BUT WE CANNOT FILL YOUR ORDER AS RECEIVED. YOUR BOOK TITLE "AN INTRODUCTION TO HIEROGLYPHICS" IS NOT CURRENTLY IN STOCK.

WE ARE ENCLOSING A REFUND CHECK IN THE AMOUNT OF $2,000.-00. PLEASE REFER TO ORDER NO. 00080766 IN ANY FUTURE CORRESPONDENCE. THANK YOU FOR SHOPPING AT WORLD BOOKS.

World Books
18 West 38th St.
NYC 10015

Feb. 24, 1988
102 East 22nd St.
NYC 10010

Just a note of thanks for your timely refund in regard to Order No. 00080766. It was much more generous than I had anticipated. I used it to clean up some credit-card debt accumulated over the holidays, and also to sign up for a set of Tai Chi lessons.

> Warmest personal regards,
> Donny

P.S. My mother enjoyed the book thoroughly and had a great trip. She's thinking about China next year.

TO   : MR. D. SHEE
REF ORDER NO. : 00080766
DATE   : 03/15/88

WE ARE SORRY BUT WE CANNOT FILL YOUR ORDER AS RECEIVED. ORDER NO 00080766 HAS BEEN FILLED OR REFUNDED AND DEACTIVATED. THANK YOU FOR SHOPPING AT WORLD BOOKS.

World Books
18 West 38th St.
NYC 10015

March 20, 1988
102 East 22nd St.
NYC 10010

I was saddened to learn that Order No. 00080766 has been deactivated. Order numbers don't come much better.
   Still, I understand your position. Nothing is forever.
   I look forward to shopping at World Books again soon.

> Till then. I will assuredly remain,
> D. Shee

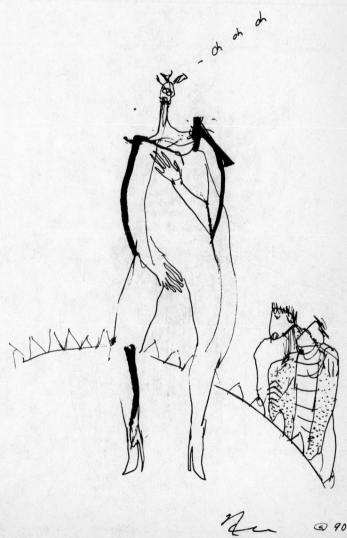

Up here in northern Alberta doing the same kind of gig I was doing in Saskatchewan—only this place is *really* isolated—and only twelve people—way out in the bush—a retreat more than a workshop—it's absolutely Cistercian, no smoking, no alcohol—there is nothing but the Silence of the Tomb—people eat in a sort of dainty hush at meals—there was an explosion of maniacal howling down in the draw of the river just behind the lodge today—it was a coyote pack, bizarre soprano shrieks, also like feedback sounds or high-frequency radio static—coyotes will kill dogs—my first thought was that they were dismembering Harpo and celebrating the fact—they were so *close*—yards away—and we all went off looking for him—no Harpo—looked up and down this river for hours. This river is peculiar—brown as coffee, and also it cuts through a four-foot coal seam, coal lying around in chunks, coal on the shore in pieces as big as your head, a black stripe through the bank—I mean, you could sit there and set the stuff on fire with your lighter—bits of coal mixed in with all this glacial till—and pieces of petrified trees, too—& no Harpo— but more wild coyote shrieking always just out of reach and a dense, dense forest and bushes and *things*—we looked for six hours and came back and he was sitting in the car where I'd left him when I went to town to get cigarettes. And forgot to let him out. They have a good library here—I found an old *New Directions,* where Merton first published "The Early Legend"—he was a damned genius and remember how uncool it was to be a monk back then?—and Eastlake's *A Child's Garden of Verses for the Revolution,* 1969 (?) edition, and here I'd never read it! Spent ten days in Nelson painting the house and then had to split for here—did I tell you Brother Emory read the epigraph from *Blackwater* at the funeral? By supper this evening everybody started to warm up and people started making trifle jokes—trifle is this English sort of stuff that Canadians eat, with cake and jam—some people disagree on the jam—Canadian humor, eh? but I laughed till my face hurt—the best one was *As I Lay Trifling,* but there was also *Mary, Trifle of Scots,* and I scored with *Gone with the Trifle,* and all in all you had to be there. All along the river today I was also looking at the pieces of coal, because sometimes they've got fossil leaves or insects in them, something preserved and exact, messages from the dead—and whatever they say, you have to listen, like it or not. **Q**

Dear Recreation Director;

God Bless you for the beautiful radio I won at your recent Senior — Citizens Luncheon.

I am 84 years old and I live at the County Home for the Aged, my people are gone and its nice to know some one like you thinks about me.

God Bless You for your kindness to an old Forgotten lady.

My roommate is 96 and always had her own radio but she wouldn't ever let me listen to it. The other day her radio fell and broke into a million pieces. it was awful and she asked me if she could listen to mine and I said fuck you.

Sincerely,
Enid Crackel

He was no longer
using his head

FOR CREDIT-CARD ORDERS OF BACK NUMBERS, CALL TOLL-FREE, AT 1-800-733-3000. PRICES AND ISBN CODES SHOWN BELOW. OR PURCHASE BY CHECK OR MONEY ORDER VIA LETTER TO SUBSCRIPTION OFFICE. NOTE ADDITION OF POSTAGE AND HANDLING CHARGE AT $1.50 THE COPY PER EACH COPY REQUESTED.

Q1	$6.95	394-74697-X
Q2	$5.95	394-74698-8
Q3	$5.95	394-75536-7
Q4	$5.95	394-75537-5
Q5	$6.95	394-75718-1
Q6	$6.95	394-75719-X
Q7	$6.95	394-75936-2
Q8	$6.95	394-75937-0
Q9	$7.95	679-72139-8
Q10	$7.95	679-72172-X
Q11	$7.95	679-72173-8
Q12	$7.95	679-72153-3